CANCEL ALL OUR VOWS

Mount Olivet: An Impression by Peter F. Anson

BROCARD SEWELL

Cancel all our Vows
BROTHER JOSEPH GARD'NER AND
THE SERVANTS OF CHRIST THE KING

'Cancel all our vows . . . '
MICHAEL DRAYTON, Sonnet lxi

The
Aylesford
Press

FIRST PUBLISHED 1988 BY
THE AYLESFORD PRESS

COPYRIGHT © 1988 BROCARD SEWELL
FOREWORD COPYRIGHT © 1988 A.N. WILSON
APPENDIX 2 COPYRIGHT © 1988 RONALD ANDERSON
DRAWING BY PETER F. ANSON COPYRIGHT © THE ABBEY OF NUNRAW
OTHER ILLUSTRATIONS COPYRIGHT © THE MORE HOUSE SCHOOL

British Library Cataloguing in Publication Data

Sewell, Brocard
Cancel all our vows.
1. Society of Christ the King. Gard'ner, Joseph
I. Title
255' .79
ISBN 1-86995-507-2
ISBN 1-86995-506-4 Pbk

PRINTED IN GREAT BRITAIN
BLOOMFIELD AND SON
STRATFORD-UPON-AVON, WARWICKSHIRE
BOUND IN GREAT BRITAIN
THOMAS LOUGHLIN
LIVERPOOL, MERSEYSIDE

TO
DONALD HALLIDAY

AUTHOR'S NOTE

THIS MEMOIR is a study in the religious life, that is, the life of dedication and community, lived under the three vows. It is also a footnote, as it were, to the long story of monastic life in England. The lives of monks, friars, nuns, and other such supposed anachronisms seem to hold a fascination for the public, whether believers or not. Monasteries have always harboured unusual personalities, most of them destined to remain unknown outside their communities. Brother Joseph Gard'ner was a religious who never rose high in the church; in the 1930s he enjoyed a brief period of relative fame, only to lapse back into obscurity after his early death in 1947. His story is worth recording, and illustrates the fact that the byways of the ecclesiastical scene are sometimes more captivating than the better known highways. I had the distinction of being the last novice admitted to Brother Joseph's community, the Servants of Christ the King; but I could not have hoped to tell his story at all adequately without the help of others; most especially that of Mr Donald Halliday, himself a surviving witness of some of these scenes and episodes, whose memory is very retentive, and whose judgement is always well weighed.

I am also greatly indebted to Mr Wilfrid Hall, Mr W. Gilmoure, the Reverend D.J. Dermott, Mr J.C. James, the Reverend Charles Borelli, Mr A.W. Campbell, Monsignor J.D. Crichton, Mr F. Cyril Hurst, and Dom Simon Bowery, OSB. For research assistance I must thank Dr Margaret M. Maison and Ms Jennifer Mackilligin.

I am very grateful to Mr S.M. Mullen, Head Master of More House School, for his hospitality in receiving me and giving his valuable time. I was able to examine the Joseph Gard'ner archive, and he very kindly and generously arranged for the reproduction of a poster and three photographs, included here with his permission.

For information relating to the late Father William Wyber I am indebted to the late Right Reverend Dr George Simms, formerly Archbishop of Dublin, and to Mr Ronald Anderson. I am especially grateful to the Reverend Michael Clifton, archivist to the Latin-rite diocese of Southwark, for kindly supplying me with documents in his care; and I am similarly indebted to the Abbot of Prinknash and Dom Sylvester Houédard, OSB.

For permission to reproduce the late Mr Peter Anson's drawing of Mount Olivet Monastery I am greatly obliged to the Abbot of Sancta Maria Abbey, Nunraw, the Right Reverend Donald McGlynn, OCSO. And it is a pleasure to thank my confrère, Fr Richard Copsey, of the Carmelite Order, for accompanying me, and providing transport, on brief visits to Frensham and Pershore.

Finally, I must acknowledge the kindness of Mr A.N. Wilson, so notable a connoisseur of the clerical scene, in contributing his elegant Foreword.

Brocard Sewell

CONTENTS

ILLUSTRATIONS

FOREWORD

ONE OF THE IMAGES from this remarkable memoir which will always remain with me is the picture of a man wearing a religious habit and a top hat, presiding as a ringmaster at a circus, of his own devising, at which the performers are mentally retarded.

It seems emblematic of Brother Joseph Gard'ner's whole life. On the one hand, the story which follows is that of a remarkable religious figure, who not only did much to foster the spiritual life in the two churches to which he belonged, but also, in his Roman Catholic existence did much good practical work with disabled boys. On the other hand, there is the top hat and the habit—the essential incompatibility which is the essence of farce.

Who better to tell the story of Brother Joseph's short life but Father Brocard Sewell. He is a tremendous rescuer of lost reputations. He has great warmth of heart. He is more profoundly knowledgeable about the by-ways of church life than any other historian. And he is one of the sharpest, wittiest writers alive today.

Cancel all our Vows takes us through the familiar never-never land of early twentieth century Anglo-Catholicism, but with a cast of unfamiliar characters. We follow the fortunes of Reg Gardner as, by various leaps of piety and imagination, he turns himself into Brother Joseph Gard'ner (how important the apostrophe was to him) kitting out the Shrine of Christ the King with lovely Spanish vestments from Mr Bartlett's shop opposite Westminster Cathedral. Happy days.

The scene of his 'awakening', when, in the course of a sermon preached to a large crowd of pilgrims and the Abbot of Nashdom, he hears himself denouncing the very movement to which he and they have given their lives has a weird kind of tragi-comedy. But it is symptomatic of the strange schizophrenia which is—or at any rate was—Anglo-Catholicism.

This violent onslaught of Roman fever could only be cured by crossing the Tiber. And it is there that as a young novice, Brocard Sewell himself met and lived with Brother Joseph. He is uniquely well-placed to describe the final debacle.

Like many remarkable people, Brother Joseph Gard'ner was destined to live only a short time on this earth. Reading Father Brocard's account, we realise that he crammed more into his thirty-nine years than most men put into ninety—'good measure, pressed down, and shaken together, and running over'.

A.N. Wilson

THE STORY OF THE SERVANTS OF CHRIST THE KING and of Mount Olivet Monastery is essentially the story of Reginald Joseph Gardner, later known as the Reverend Brother Joseph Gard'ner. He was born on 9 July 1908 at 19 London Road, Bracknell, near Reading. His father, Frank Gardner, was at the time a grocer's assistant. His mother was Annie Elizabeth Gardner, formerly North. Frank Gardner sang in the Bracknell parish church choir, and had something of a reputation as a soloist. He and his wife were both Low Church in their religious beliefs and practice. The family seems to have lived in Berkshire for a good period of time. In 1937 Brother Joseph pointed out to a companion as they were driving through Reading the classical portico and tower of St. Mary's, Castle Street, of which he remarked that it was the 'lowest' Church of England church in Reading, adding that his grandfather had been a regular worshipper there all his life.

In later life Reginald Gardner spelled his surname 'Gard'ner'; the apostrophe seems to have been of his own invention, and was probably intended to add a desirably romantic, perhaps even aristocratic note to his respectable but somewhat prosaic patronymic.

At some point during his childhood his parents moved for a time to Yorkshire, where they lived quite close to the Community of the Resurrection at Mirfield; it was here, in the chapel of the Mirfield community, that Reginald Gardner acquired his Anglo-Catholicism, and his love of church ritual.

In his Yorkshire home, when he was perhaps seven or eight, Reg, as his parents called him, and his young friends were allowed to use the dining room sideboard as an improvised altar, with lighted candles, at which they enacted the rite of Benediction. Low Church though his parents may have been, they were evidently not narrow-minded.

Unfortunately, we have no information about Reginald's schooling, most of which he is believed to have received in Reading. In later years he showed every sign of being an educated man, but he did not appear to have read very widely or deeply. His parents' lack of means would probably have prevented his going to university, even on a scholarship; but it is doubtful if his education reached that level. He left school quite early, and seems to have sprung onto life's stage—no inapt metaphor—almost a fully fledged adult. Having left school at sixteen or seventeen, he went straight into the theatre as his chosen career. The sum of our knowledge enables us to deduce with certainty that from his childhood, continuing through his schooldays, he delighted in amateur theatricals, for which he showed unusual talent.

On leaving school he succeeded in attaching himself, almost as a latter-day 'strolling player', to one or more of the small companies of actors and actresses that toured the seaside resorts, especially during the summer. On the playbills his name appeared as Rex Lynn Linton. He probably 'borrowed' this *nom de guerre* from that of the once famous Victorian novelist Eliza Lynn Linton. Perhaps he had come across her two best-selling novels, *Joshua Davidson* and *Autobiography of Christopher Kirkland*. Many years later he told his friend Jim Bowery that during these seaside engagements he was always accompanied, and carefully chaperoned, by his mother, who kept him under a strict surveillance. This was no small trial to him, as it would be to any sixteen- or seventeen-year-old. 'Bowery,' he was once moved to say, 'you have no *idea* how awful it was!'

Before long, however, he had graduated from seaside piers to a place with the Leeds Repertory Theatre Company, where he was free of his mother's oversight. Unfortunately, it has proved impossible to trace his acting career since the British Actors' Equity Association was formed as recently as 1932, and has no earlier records of members of the profession. But his career on the stage was of brief duration; by the time he was nineteen he had left the theatre, bent upon making a new career in the Church. This was something that he seems never to have spoken about, and we do not know what impelled him to make this seemingly unlikely decision. He was evidently an ambitious young man, and he may have come to the conclusion that his talents as an actor were not quite sufficient to enable him to rise to the top of the tree. It was always, throughout his life, necessary for him to hold the centre of the stage, without competition from rival stars. There must have been other, more serious and more conscious, reasons behind this decision; but they can only be guessed at.

What is strange, though, is that in opting for a life of religion he seems to have had no desire for priesthood. His rather limited education would have been more of an obstacle then to acquiring holy orders than it would be now; but another difficulty may have been lack of financial support. His hope and intention was to found a new religious order, within the Anglican communion, a community of lay preaching brothers, modelled to some extent on the Dominicans, or Blackfriars, founded by St Dominic in the 13th century. As a religious founder he would always be in a prominent position, and sure of being held in special regard.

As a preliminary step he applied to the Archbishop of York for admission as a licensed lay reader. A lay reader in the Church of England must be a man of known probity, sufficient education, and devotion. There is a short course of training; a good knowledge of the Bible is required. A prescribed course of reading in divinity and church history has to be followed, and there is some training in homilectics. A lay reader can take all church services except those requiring the ministration of a priest. He can preach (except at celebrations of the Holy Communion), catechize children, visit the sick, and take charge of a parish's youth and other activities.

Once licensed as a lay reader, Reg Gard'ner, as he now spelled his name, seems to have obtained from the Archbishop of York some kind of general approval or blessing for his project of founding a community of preaching brothers. To this end he designed for himself a grey monastic habit, more Franciscan than Dominican in pattern, and bestowed on himself the religious name of Brother Joseph of the Holy Family. This rather elaborate kind of nomenclature was a device popular with reformed religious communities of the Counter-Reformation era (Carmelites, Trinitarians, and others). It was still in force among the Discalced Carmelites until quite recently. However, Brother Joseph seems not to have made much use of his cognomen, and in fact it was soon dropped.

An entirely original touch was the bright red cord girdle that he prescribed to be worn with the grey habit; for this there was really no precedent, the nearest thing to it, the cord girdle worn by the members of the Society of the Sacred Mission being plum-coloured rather than red.

Seeing that the grey habit was so Franciscan in character, it was really a great pity that Brother Joseph, as we must now call him, had a strong dislike for Franciscans and Franciscanism, how acquired we can only guess.

Nineteen was an early age at which to set up as a religious founder; but there is no need to doubt Brother Joseph's seriousness of purpose, and sincerity. He had no qualifications whatever for this high and serious mission beyond his dedication and enthusiasm. Of training in the ways of the religious life he had had none. He should, of course, have spent some time with one of the established Anglican communities, if not as a member then at least as some kind of internal observer. Brother Joseph, however, preferred to follow the example of an earlier Anglican pioneer, the Reverend Joseph Leycester Lyne (Father Ignatius of Llanthony), who set up his neo-Benedictine abbey at Capel-y-ffin in 1870 without himself having received any monastic training. Brother Joseph must have known of this ill-fated venture, and should have taken warning from it. But he was an intensely self-willed, self-confident, and determined young man, and preferred to do things his own way.

Brother Joseph's Anglo-Catholicism had by now developed well beyond the standard of the Community of the Resurrection, which had so strongly influenced him during his childhood. He was now an out and out Papalist, believing not only that the Church of England is 'the Catholic church of this land', but that its separation from its mother-church in Rome is a scandal crying out to be put right as soon as possible. Reunion is thus a matter of urgency. The position is well and cogently argued, with a wealth of learning, by the Reverend Spencer Jones in his book *England and the Holy See*. In general, Anglo-Papalists at that time accepted all the decrees of the Council of Trent and of the Vatican Council of 1870. Inevitably, many from within their ranks seceded to the mother church; but those who remained loyal to the See of Canterbury or York thought that such individual secessions did little or nothing to remedy the anomalous situation of the English Church; the right way was to work and pray for *corporate* reunion.

In the churches of the papalist clergy there was little difference between the services held there and those held in Roman Catholic churches; in some 'advanced' churches the Mass, or at least the Canon of the Mass, was said or sung in Latin; in others it was just a matter of the *Missale Romanum* as translated in Knott and Company's *The English Missal*. The Book of Common Prayer was very little in evidence, and its use was not encouraged. The evening service of Benediction of the Blessed Sacrament—strongly disapproved of by most Anglican bishops—was held to be an essential feature of 'Catholic' worship; devotion to the Blessed Virgin Mary was encouraged by means of the rosary, novenas of prayer to Our Lady of Perpetual Succour, and other 'Roman' devotions.

Such was Brother Joseph's standpoint in 1927, when he contrived for himself a position as lay reader in the Yorkshire parish of Hinderwell. The rector, the Reverend Arthur Middleton Bolland, MA, was an archetypal country parson, benign, erudite, a moderate high churchman, liked and respected by all. Mr Bolland had no particular interest in religious orders, but he was always ready to encourage initiatives that seemed likely to advance the cause of religion; so he was sympathetic and understanding towards Brother Joseph's plans for the founding of a fraternity of preaching brothers.

The parish of Hinderwell, near Saltburn, had, and still has, a mission church, or chapel-of-ease in the nearby fishing village of Staithes, and of this chapel Brother Joseph was put in charge. A survivor from those days, who was a boy at the time, says that 'Brother Joseph descended on Staithes like a being from outer space.' The *Handbook* of the Automobile Association describes Staithes as 'a picturesque village in a bay encircled by lofty cliffs. There is sand at low tide, and also bathing. The descent from the main road has a gradient of 1 in 5.' In the late 1920s the village was just beginning to struggle out of the insularity of generations, and was probably a full decade behind the nearest urban communities. There was no gas or electricity, very few houses had even a cold-water tap indoors, and outdoor earth-closets provided the only sanitation. There is a good account of the village as it was in Dame Laura Knight's autobiography, *The Magic of a Line*. Dame Laura and her husband, Harold Knight, RA, lived in Staithes for fourteen years. She gives no dates, but since the Knights moved to Cornwall in or about 1912 it is clear that they were in Staithes a good while before Brother Joseph; but present-day residents are agreed that the place will have changed very little between 1912 and Brother Joseph's arrival in 1927.

In her book Laura Knight's chapter on Staithes has the title 'A Wildified Place', and she calls the villagers 'proud fisher-people'. These fisher-folk are said to be descended from some Northern race of Viking people, whose vessel had been wrecked on that piece of shore many centuries ago. Their life was full of hazards, and so were the lives of their descendants. Dame Laura recalls being woken up early one morning by the sound of a woman wailing: a terrifying sound. Later, at low tide, the body of the woman's father was found washed up on a beach to the north of the village. It was recovered, and brought back to his cottage, where it was placed on a table spread for the wedding feast of one of his sons. The white table cloth became his winding sheet.

'The autumn tang of breeze', Dame Laura writes, 'embraces one's cheek with a bristly kiss. On the shadowed Staithe—the quay, running parallel to the shore—old men crouch on their hunkers and search their trouser pockets for a taste of "baccy"; wives pull their knitting needles from holders at the waist. Click, click, click, they sound, as women in groups gossip and automatically knit blue jerseys for their men-folk. All eyes watch the cobbles [fishing boats] vanish. No matter how calm the sea this hour, the beaches may be strewn with wreckage tomorrow.'

In 1927 housing conditions in Staithes were primitive. The men had a hard life at sea, the women a hard life at home. Brother Joseph, whose health was not good—he was a life-long asthmatic—had no hesitations about sharing these rough living-conditions. He and his first two companions lived in a small four-roomed cottage with all the disadvantages we have described, and with no patch of garden, nor any proper back-yard. He had no salary—presumably the parish was too poor to provide one: he and his companions seem to have been supported by the generosity of the villagers and by whatever donations Brother Joseph might secure from outside sources. The furnishings of St Francis's Cottage—as their dwelling was oddly named, but perhaps Brother Joseph admired St Francis more than he did Franciscans or Franciscanism—were austere in the extreme; no coverings on the wooden floors, just a plain deal table and some chairs in the living room, and plank beds.

Brother Joseph quickly became part of the village life. The mission-church was actually an upper room in an old stone-built church school. The services here were traditionally of a 'normal' kind, and the Rector's scholarly sermons were inclined to be soporific; although occasionally they were mildly chiding in tone. The congregation usually consisted of about twelve to fourteen adults and a few children. The Methodists actually had three chapels in the village; in addition there was the small Roman Catholic church of Our Lady Star of the Sea. I dearly wish I knew how the RCs in Staithes—there can hardly have been many of them—reacted to Brother Joseph; but on that matter history is silent.

All three Methodist chapels were well attended. Laura and Harold Knight used to frequent the chapel of the Primitive Methodists, known in the locality as 'Ranters'. The Ranters' prayer meetings could be quite exciting; for instance, when 'them as is drunkards confess, and is saaved, an' don't ever get drunk any more'. Laura Knight comments that 'This heated state of ecstasy, leading perhaps to revelation of mutual sin, did not always prove too wise.'

Under Joseph Gard'ner's charge the Mission Church of St Peter the Fisherman, as it was rather grandly styled—perhaps Brother Joseph himself gave it this dedication?—became every bit as exciting as, and even more theatrical than, 't'Ranter Chapil'. With the little spare money that he had at his disposal the Reverend Brother —this being the designation that he had bestowed on himself—at once set about transforming the rather bare and austerely furnished interior of the mission room—for really it was not much more than that—into a very fair imitation of a typical Roman Catholic church or chapel of the period, with plenty of gaudy plaster statues of saints, and a plethora of small candlesticks and flower-vases of

27

brass. The dominant colour-scheme was red and gold, these being Brother Joseph's favourite colours. Candles multiplied as if by magic; soon there were twelve on the altar, six on each side of the altar-cross, so that there seemed to be imminent danger of a conflagration. The plaster saints filled every niche and corner, and at service-time incense arose in clouds.

An old inhabitant, Mr J.C. James, recalls the first time that he saw Brother Joseph, walking up the aisle, wearing over his grey habit a lace-edged cotta. He remembers him as a small, boyish figure, with dark burning eyes, and a neat beard. Beards were at that time unconventional; but there was a practical reason for Brother Joseph's; it was grown in order to conceal a weakness of the jaw.

He quickly showed himself to be a very effective youth organizer. He involved the boys of his congregation in all sorts of activities, and had them firmly under his thumb. He even succeeded in getting them to drop into the church at odd times in order to pray. Mr James says: 'I think the only gain from this activity was that at least we weren't in any particular mischief during the few minutes we were in church.'

All this amounted to a revolution, and Brother Joseph's impassioned preaching filled the little church to capacity. At Evensong it was a matter of standing room only. The person least affected by this transformation seems to have been Mr Bolland, who continued unperturbed on his perambulations through the village, wearing a slightly bemused expression.

The late Joseph Wilson, then a young man aged seventeen, was closely involved with the church of St Peter the Fisherman, and became the first recruit to Brother Joseph's community. Born in 1910, he came from a farming family near Whitby, but lived in the country a mile or so outside Staithes. In the community he was known as Brother Francis. He stayed with Brother Joseph until the early 1930s, moving with him from Staithes to Pershore, and then to Frensham, in Surrey. Probably he was with Brother Joseph for something like five years, a much longer time than the average novice survived.

It used to be said of Father Benedict Williamson, the architect-monk who tried to re-found the extinct male branch of the Bridgettine

Order, that the reason why he could never keep any novices was that he was too holy for them. This was hardly the case with Brother Joseph, who was an impatient and irascible man; but there can be no doubt at all that he was able to inspire devotion. It says much for Brother Francis's tenacity and seriousness of purpose that he lasted so long. Eventually, however, he left the community and married. In later years he would often speak of his time with Brother Joseph, of which he kept happy memories.

Quite apart from his ritualistic church services and his fiery sermons, Brother Joseph showed in other ways that he was a gifted actor and impresario. Mr James says: 'I still remember the Passion Play he produced, and of course starred in. With most unlikely actors. To me the atmosphere was electric, and even now that night was the nearest I have ever been to the Passion.'

And then, quite suddenly, less than two years later, it was all over. Brother Joseph, Brother Francis, and another novice who had been recruited, vanished; and were not seen again in those parts.

What had brought this about? In Staithes today it seems to be a matter of speculation; no one remembers the precise circumstances. However, Brother Anthony, one of the later members of the community, knew the facts, which he had perhaps heard from Brother Francis.

One of Brother Joseph's activities in Staithes was open-air preaching: in the streets or on the Staithe (the quay). It was this open-air preaching that brought about his downfall. When preaching out of doors Brother Joseph was always accompanied by one or other of his companions, and held in his left hand what he called his preaching cross. This was a tall wooden cross, brightly painted in red and gold. The spectacle of some kind of monk preaching in the open naturally intrigued those of the young people, mainly boys, of Staithes who did not worship at the church of St Peter the Fisherman; their reaction was mostly one of friendly mockery rather than of devotion. In fact, these small boys proved a considerable hindrance to Brother Joseph's efforts to convert the people of Staithes to the true religion. He was not a patient man, and could not put up with heckling and teasing for very long. In an unfortunate hour his small stock of patience quite forsook him, and he sought to belabour his young tormentors with the sacred symbol of our salvation. The ensuing commotion quickly brought the indignant village fish-wives and mothers to the aid of their offspring. The two Brothers had to retreat quickly to their cottage in order to save themselves. After that, it was felt best by all concerned that Brother Joseph and his little community should seek some other sphere of activity. The popish furnishings of the church of St Peter the Fisherman were swiftly removed, and the services reverted to their previous gentle torpor.

Nevertheless, Brother Joseph had made his mark at Staithes, and had shown something of what he was capable of. And it was at Staithes that the future direction of his life and work began to be made clear.

Not long after he had arrived in Staithes, in 1927, a visiting clergyman had given him a small white plaster statue, about eight inches high, of Christ the King. This little figure of a standing Christ, robed and crowned, was of the Beuronese school of art, and seems to have come from the Benedictine abbey of Maria Laach, in the Rhineland. Strange to say, Brother Joseph seems not yet to have heard of the new devotion to the Kingship of Christ, promulgated only two years before by Pope Pius XI in his encyclical letter *Quas primas*. The Reverend Brother was at once captivated by it, and resolved that the principal mission of his community, which he then and there named the Servants of Christ the King, should be to spread this devotion.

The cataclysmic episode of the preaching cross probably occurred in the summer or autumn of 1930; but already Brother Joseph had been thinking of leaving Staithes, and transferring to a more accessible area, where he would be closer to the mainstream of church life; an area also with a greater potential for attracting recruits to the order. In the spring of 1930 he had been visiting the Reverend Spencer Jones at Moreton-in-Marsh, Gloucestershire, where one afternoon he saw a small party of black-habited monks getting out of a car and going into a nearby hotel. Curious as to who they might be, he followed them in and introduced himself. They were monks from the Anglican Benedictine community at Nashdom Abbey, near Burnham, and were on their way home after a visit to their former monastery at Pershore, which was now empty. The leader of the party was Dom Martin Collett, to whom Brother Joseph described the difficult conditions under which he and his companions were living in Staithes. Dom Martin was interested and sympathetic, and said that he thought his superior, Abbot Denys Prideaux, might perhaps be persuaded to lend the empty Abbey House at Pershore, near Worcester, to the Servants of Christ the King, at least as a temporary abode. This was duly arranged, and at the end of December Brother Joseph and Brother Francis moved into the Abbey House. On 2 January 1931 they were joined by two novices, and a third arrived later in the month.

The ancient and picturesque town of Pershore offered a livelier and more varied scene than remote Staithes, but the community's life at Pershore was scarcely less austere. The Abbey House was only a kind of glorified farmhouse built at the end of the last century, and was quite unsuitable for housing a monastic community. It was a decaying and uncomfortable building, far from weather-proof. The life of the community remained distinctly penitential.

To coincide with the arrival there of the Brothers was published the first number of *Christus Rex*, the magazine that was to be the official organ of the Servants of Christ the King, and Brother Joseph's principal means of keeping in touch with his supporters. The Community Notes in this first number, which had four pages only, say that 'A number of very kind gifts have made our few sticks of furniture look a little less lonely in the vastness of the Abbey, but we still need chairs, tables, linen, china, and furnishings for the chapel.'

At Pershore the founder-superior of the SCK, and his companions, were admitted as oblates of Nashdom Abbey, and the way of life was restructured on a pattern of mild Benedictinism. *Christus Rex* reports that 'the Divine Office is once more offered in the Abbey'. These services were probably based on an English translation of the Day Hours of the Church, from the *Diurnum Monasticum*. As an outward sign of this reorientation the Brotherhood's red cord girdle was put aside—not very willingly on Brother Joseph's part, one may be sure—and a black cord substituted. They were now, as Brother Joseph explained, 'a modern congregation with a rule based on the experience of the great monastic orders, but not claiming to be part of the older monastic families . . . I do not think it is possible to be either a Franciscan or a Dominican in the English Church, since they are an entirely papal organization—as distinct from the Benedictine family which came into being before the schism'. The Abbot of Nashdom accepted the more or less honorary position of Warden of the Community, and assigned Dom Martin Collett as its spiritual director. Although non-resident, Dom Martin took his responsibilities seriously, and was a frequent visitor.

The original conception of the community as a band of preaching brothers was dropped; but Brother Joseph himself continued to accept invitations to preach, for by now he had made a considerable name for himself in that direction. In fact, as a preacher he was much in demand. He obviously enjoyed preaching, in spite of occasional embarrassments when his troublesome jaw dropped and became fixed, so that he had to give it a resounding blow to get it back into place. In the last months of the year 1930 he had secured for himself over twenty invitations to preach and address meetings all over England. Frequently he was allowed to make pulpit appeals on behalf of his Community, and would come away with generous collections. Since no one else in the community had any real earning power, or at best very little, these preaching engagements were necessary for its survival. It was principally through them that Brother Joseph and the SCK became a well-known and popular feature of the Anglo-Catholic scene.

One of several London churches in which the Brother Superior was invited to preach was St Giles's, Pentonville, where he briefly joined forces with the well-known Brother Edward (the Reverend E. Bulstrode) in a campaign of street evangelism. As a young man Edward Bulstrode had handed over his share in his father's estate to his employees; then, with no further possessions than the clothes he stood up in, he took to the roads as an itinerant missioner. A frail, bearded figure in a cassock, he lived the life of a primitive Franciscan, eventually founding the Evangelist Brothers of Jesus of Nazareth. Unfortunately, the partnership between Brother Edward and Brother Joseph was not the success that had been expected; the two evangelists fell out, and walked no more together. Which was

Brother Joseph Gard'ner

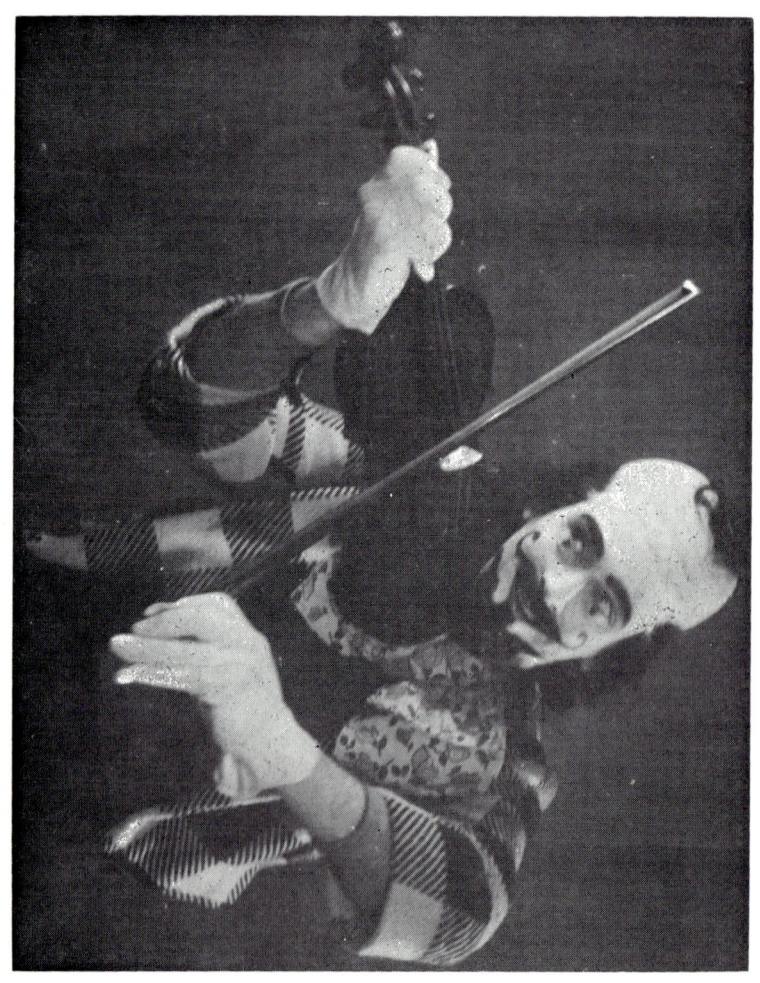

Brother Joseph as a circus clown

a pity, for Brother Edward, an older and more experienced man, and a clergyman too, might have been expected to supply the kind of spiritual guidance that the younger man so greatly needed.

Back at Pershore, as the first number of *Christus Rex* records, there had been set up a 'Fellowship of Help', with two simple obligations: to pray daily for the community, and to help it how and when the members could. The Patrons of the Fellowship of Help were the Lord Abbot of Pershore and Nashdom, the Prior of Alton (of the Order of St Paul), and the Reverend the Viscount Mountmorres. The secretary and administrator to the Fellowship of Help was the Reverend John Robert Sankey. Father Sankey, formerly of Ely Theological College and Pembroke College, Oxford, was ordained in 1907, served a variety of curacies in the diocese, and in 1923 was appointed Rector of St Andrew-by-the-Wardrobe with St Anne's, Blackfriars. After which there seems to be no clear record of his career. Perhaps he was something of a rolling stone who had attached himself temporarily to the Servants of Christ the King as acting chaplain.

There were now five Brothers in the community; perhaps as many as there ever would be at any point of its existence; but there was no prospect of their being allowed to do any work in connexion with the parish. After the dissolution of the monastery at Pershore in 1534 the abbey buildings had been destroyed, and the nave of the abbey church also. The townsfolk paid £400 to save the choir and transepts, which today serve as the parish church. It is a splendid, rather 'chunky' building, dating from A.D. 972 onwards: but the impressive flying buttresses are Victorian. Unfortunately for Brother Joseph, in 1931 the parish had a low church vicar, who was not sympathetic to monasticism. He is known to have expressed pleasure at the departure of the ex-Caldey monks (the Pershore-Nashdom community), so he can hardly have welcomed their replacement by the SCK. Happily there was enough manual work in the semi-ruinous Abbey House and its garden to keep the Brothers occupied. Among other activities, they operated a small printing press, and repaired damaged statues and crucifixes. *Christus Rex* mentions ST ANTHONY'S BAKEHOUSE: 'that part of our financial work which consists of the distribution and selling of Novices'

33

Bread Tickets.' Readers were invited to write for a Bread Box: presumably some kind of collecting-box towards the cost of feeding the novices. St Anthony's Bakehouse was obviously an adaptation of the St Anthony's Bread alms-boxes for offerings for the poor that are to be seen in Roman Catholic churches.

It was plain, however, that if the community was to grow and prosper some more specific form or forms of apostolic activity would have to be found for the Brothers. *Christus Rex* speaks hopefully but vaguely of 'plans for some educational work'.

In the end it was Dom Martin Collett who provided the solution to this problem. Dom Martin was the spiritual director of the Sisters of the Transfiguration, an Anglican community founded in 1918 by the Reverend A.H. Baverstock, Rector of Hinton Martell in Dorset, and Miss Stone (Sister Mary Frances). In 1928 these Sisters had taken over an old workhouse in Basingstoke, which they renamed Mount Tabor and opened as a home for fifty mentally defective girls. The Abbot of Nashdom was the Visitor to this Community, and its Warden was the scholar-monk Dom Gregory Dix. The Sisters followed the Holy Rule of St Benedict. It was through Dom Martin Collett that the Superior of the Sisters of the Transfiguration suggested to Brother Joseph that the Servants of Christ the King should take up similar work, but for mentally defective boys.

During the negotiations it was necessary for Brother Joseph to consult Father Baverstock, who had living in his rectory at Hinton Martell four or five mentally defective boys for whom he was caring. Helping him in this work was John Fuller, a young man who was later to join the SCK and become one of Brother Joseph's most trusted collaborators. Brother Joseph was also taken to see Sister Mary Frances, at Basingstoke, who a little later was able to tell him that she had found a property, at Frensham, in Surrey, that would be very suitable for his purpose. At that point removal from Pershore was resolved on.

Announcing this, *Christus Rex* for April 1931 said: 'We hope to receive between twenty and thirty boys... who are sufficiently feeble-minded to require care and control, but who are capable of doing garden work, weaving, boot repairing, mat making, and similar work under supervision ... The devil would like to see our community fail for lack of support—let your motto be "A penny a day keeps the devil away." '

The move to Frensham began in July, and the community was fully settled in by August 16th. The Brothers had been in Pershore just over six months. They seem to have made little impression on the ancient town. No one there today remembers them. The *Short History of Pershore* published in 1972 makes no mention of them, nor do the contemporary numbers of the local paper, *Berrow's Worcester Journal*. At Frensham in later years it was remembered that at Pershore the Brothers had sometimes held outdoor processions, with the Superior bringing up the rear and carrying the Beuronese statue of Christ the King. These must have been very humble little processions, perhaps confined to the garden of the Abbey House, or to the precincts of the former abbey church.

It is perhaps significant of certain later developments, which we shall record in due course, that when the *Nashdom Abbey Jubilee Book (1914-1964)* was published in 1964 the only reference to Brother Joseph (who is not named) and his community was a brief sentence recording the lending for a time of the Abbey House at Pershore 'to a somewhat ephemeral body known as "The Community of Christ the King" '.

The property which Sister Mary Frances had found for the Servants of Christ the King was situated on Moon's Hill in the parish of Frensham, three miles or so from the Hampshire town of Farnham. The house, a large and impressive brick structure, with Italianate features, is thought to have been built as an hotel. In July 1972 it was partly destroyed by fire; although the damage has been made good, the house is not quite so impressive today as formerly it was, in spite of extensions and additions that have been made to it since. The whole property comprised also fourteen acres of land, and a further small block of buildings which Brother Joseph named St Anthony's and St Joseph's Cottages. The spacious grounds include a large, steeply-terraced garden. From the loggia of the house, and from the terraces, there is a superb view over three counties.

Christus Rex for September 1931 says that some goats have been acquired, and that there are hopes of starting a poultry farm. It is intended to build a grotto of Christ the King 'as a pilgrimage centre'.

35

There is an appeal for gifts of furniture, books, pictures, linen and blankets, garden implements, seeds and bulbs. 'The demand for Bread Tickets has not been so keen this [sic] last few months.'

Pilgrimages of devotion soon became a principal feature of life at Mount Olivet Monastery, as the house had been renamed, in compliment to Mount Tabor at Woking. Pilgrims began to come in ever-increasing numbers, especially in big groups from Anglo-Catholic churches in London. These pious outings took place mostly on the principal church festivals. The pilgrims were generous—as pilgrims to popular shrines always are—and their offerings became an important factor in the development of the Monastery and Shrine, and of the Institution for boys. The new Monastery was solemnly blessed by the Bishop of Guildford, Dr John Harold Greig, on the Vigil of Christ the King, 24 October. On the same day the new chapel of Christ the King was opened. In this chapel was placed the image which was to be the centre or focus of the pilgrim's devotions.

It was a rather plain little chapel, a temporary affair only. It was soon replaced by a larger ground-floor room on the west side of the house, which was more elaborately furnished. Part of the loggia was closed off to make a narrow shrine in which was placed a robed and crowned statue of Christ the King seated in majesty. This was a small, rather highly-coloured statue, probably obtained from Messrs Vanpoulle's, the London church furnishers. Later, Brother Joseph took a dislike to it because, so he said, it bore a strong facial resemblance to King Charles the Martyr. It is strange to reflect that Brother Joseph's High Anglicanism did not extend to belief in the divine right of kings and the cult of the Royal Martyr. So this statue was in due time replaced by another, of German Benedictine origin, which was acquired from Brother Joseph's now favourite source of supply, the Art and Book Company's shop in Ashley Place, immediately facing Westminster Cathedral.

In the days of the 'Charles the First' statue the background to the shrine was heavily draped in red velvet. Two or three hanging lamps were always burning before it, and there was a stand for the votive candles of the faithful.

Soon after the inauguration of the Monastery the thirty boys for whom the Brothers were to care arrived, and the Institution licensed under the Mental Deficiency Act by the Board of Control came into being. The community was now described as being under the direction of the Benedictines of Nashdom Abbey, with the Abbot of Pershore and Nashdom as its Warden, and the Bishop of Guildford its Visitor. At first there seems to have been no resident chaplain, but Dom Martin Collett came whenever he could, and occasional help was given by other Nashdom monks, among them Dom Benedict Ley and Dom Gregory Dix.

The auguries were good. After the years of hardship and uncertainty at Staithes and Pershore, the barometer seemed set fair for a promising future. But there were hidden weaknesses. Certainly Brother Joseph had a wonderful way with boys; but, since he had embarked on his religious life at the early age of nineteen, having received no training for it whatsoever, it is not surprising that he was less successful with his community. The recruitment of postulants and novices was never satisfactory, nor was Brother Joseph a good financial administrator.

The *Chronicle* of the Servants of Christ the King recording the reception of novices, and admissions to vows, seems no longer to exist, so it is not easy to determine how many Brothers there were in the community at any given time. The Community Notes in *Christus Rex* do not record such matters. At Staithes, as we have seen, the community numbered three: Brother Joseph, Brother Francis, and a third, whose identity is uncertain. At Pershore, besides the Brother Superior and Brother Francis, there were Brother Ignatius of the Passion, Brother Bernard Plant, Brother Dominic Williamson, and Brother Benedict Hinton. Most of these seem to have moved with Brother Joseph to Frensham; but by late 1933 or early 1934 all had left, of their own accord, with the exception of Brother Ignatius who was dismissed by Brother Joseph after a disagreement between them, and went away sorrowfully. He was a tailor by trade, and came from London. He also made vestments, and was the first cook at Mount Olivet. Obviously, he was a useful man. Another member of the community, Brother Martin (Wilfrid Hall), was not professed and had the status of a *familiaris*.

The only one to remain in religious life was Dominic Williamson, who spent the rest of his life as a Benedictine laybrother at Ramsgate

Abbey.

That all of Brother Joseph's first six recruits should have left does seem to indicate that something was wrong; by the law of averages at least two should have survived to make their final and perpetual vows.

However, *Christus Rex* for January 1933 gives no indication that things are going on other than well. The magazine had now grown from its original four pages to thirty-two, and had become a well edited and well produced periodical, with interesting articles on religious and theological subjects. Its circulation had grown too, and now was about 2,500, to rise further in later years to 3,000. The number for June 1933 has an article, 'Under Pontius Pilate', by Dom Gregory Dix, written to mark the nineteenth centenary of the founding of the Christian religion. There is also an article by Dr H.S. Scott, the Rector of Oddington, who had recently published his classic work *The Eastern Churches and the Papacy*. His article is a refutation of the ideas advanced by Dr N.P. Williams in his *Northern Catholicism*, where he had argued that the Papacy is essentially a feature of Italian, or Southern Catholicism, and is not necessary to Catholicism as such. Dr Scott begins his article by saying: 'There is in some quarters a good deal of loud, and, I fear, rather ignorant talk of a "non-papal Catholicism". Now, there isn't such a thing as non-papal Catholicism.' Concluding his article, Dr Scott says that 'The great Council of Chalcedon, presided over by a legate of the Pope, Leo the Great, addressed the Pope as "the constituted interpreter to all men of the voice of Blessed Peter", proclaimed that to him was "committed the guardianship of the Vine by our Saviour", and that by his legates the Bishop of Rome had "ruled over them as the head over the members." The loyal Anglican is committed and pledged to this. He has to give to the Bishop of Rome what the primitive Church acknowledged.'

The same issue of *Christus Rex* announces a retreat for laymen to be held at Mount Olivet in September, to be conducted by the Brother Superior. There is also a report of a pilgrimage made to the shrine of Christ the King the previous Whitsun, when a High Mass was celebrated at an altar on the loggia, before an open-air congregation, the celebrant being Dom Gregory Dix. The Mass was followed by an outdoor procession, at which the statue of Christ the King was carried round the garden, and a sermon was preached by the Rector of Carshalton, Father Corbould. The pilgrimage ended with the recitation of the rosary and the singing of 'carols'— what carols?, one wonders—at the newly-built grotto of Our Lady of Lourdes.

To this exceptionally interesting issue of *Christus Rex* Brother Joseph contributed an article on 'Keeping the Laity in the Dark', in which he sounded a warning note about the danger of the purity of the Anglo-Catholic message being corrupted by High Church clergy of modernist views. 'The laity are being kept in the dark, for if they were theologians and understood one half of the heresies held by many Anglo-Catholic leaders, they would be appalled.' The writer goes on to say that 'The old-fashioned Evangelical clergyman of fifty years ago was nearer to the Catholic Truth than many clergymen of today whose external practice leads many to suppose that they are Catholics'. 'I am told', he affirms, 'that there is more than one bishop on the bench anxious to ordain women'; and there is 'an almost unbelievable but true report that a member of a religious community has occupied the pulpit in a nonconformist chapel more than once'.

Another page is filled with the announcement of a Novena to the Holy Ghost, and a Solemn Triduum to Christ the King, to be observed at the Monastery from July 27 to August 4 (St Dominic's Day). The objects of these devotional exercises are (1) Grace for the Community; (2) vocations to the Community; (3) financial aid. The Novena is to be followed on August 5, 6, and 7 by a pilgrimage and Solemn Triduum to Christ the King. Its objects are: Reparation to Christ the King, the Conversion of England, and the Restoration of Catholic Unity. The special preachers will be the Reverend E.A. Bacon, Dom Martin Collett, OSB, and the Reverend Alban Baverstock. At 9.30 a.m. on the August Bank Holiday morning a special bus will run from London (Hyde Park Corner) to the Monastery; return fare, six shillings.

The third of the Novena intentions, financial help, is significant. A summary of the Report for 1933 of the Community's auditor indicates an increase of £248 in subscriptions, as compared with the previous year; but there is still a debt of £600 on the establishment. (For present-day figures, multiply by twenty-five.) The income from grants has increased also, by £260; but on the year's running account there is a deficit of £150.

Christus Rex's number for Michaelmas 1933 carries an article by Monsignor Newsome on 'The Suggested Policy of Sterilisation'. The author was the founder of a large institution for mentally defective boys at Besford Court, in Worcestershire. Sterilisation of the 'unfit' was then a main feature in the programmes advanced by various societies advocating 'Eugenics' as a means of improving the quality of the population. A leading supporter of such 'progressive' measures was Dean Inge. Among the eugenists' principal opponents were G.K. Chesterton, Father Vincent McNabb, and the Distributist League.

In October 1933 the Servants of Christ the King published a fifty-page illustrated booklet, written by Brother Joseph: *A Comfortable Company: the Application of the Teachings of our Lord Jesus Christ in the Training of Mental Defectives*. It has a striking frontispiece: a picture of a very ectoplasmic apparition of Jesus, who is extending his hands in response to the outstretched hands of a group of shadowy boys. Under the picture are printed the words: 'Heal our Minds!'

The picture is, in fact, a photograph of Brother Joseph draped from the head downwards in a white sheet.

In his preface to the booklet Brother Joseph says that many of its readers 'will not share our views on religion, but we trust they will appreciate that but for religion we should never have attempted the work, and that, more than anything else, religion has been responsible for the development of it'.

Dr K. Waller Todd, LRCP, MRCS, who contributes an introduction to the pamphlet, heads his paragraphs with a quotation from Bunyan's *Pilgrim's Progress*: 'Then said the Shepherds, This is a comfortable company.' This quotation, Dr Todd says, has come to life in Frensham. 'Here are the strong, and those with grace shining in their faces; many a pilgrim finds his or her own way to the shrine of Christ the King and worships Him with the Brethren, His Servants. But here, too, are some who must be called in by name, some for whom liberty is for the time inadvisable; and the care of these shows the Brethren to be the Lord's shepherds indeed.' (A footnote identifies Dr Todd as a Free Churchman.)

A Comfortable Company contains a six-page essay by Brother Joseph on 'The Efficiency of Impractical Notions'. When the Brothers began the work, he says, they at first lacked trained helpers, because of their own inexperience; but this did not prove successful. They then took on men as instructors in special crafts; but these, having no knowledge of defectives, were unsuccessful also. The community still lacks in many ways the efficiency which it ought to have, but 'we are slowly building up the work on the right lines, and we have put *first things first*'. The life of the boys is largely one of trying to reach a level beyond their attainment. To offset this a life of quietness and regularity is needed, such a life as that at Mount Olivet, where the daily routine is very similar all the year round, and the life of the Monastery produces a beneficial atmosphere of stability and peace.

When the Institution commenced work in December 1931 we were faced with many problems. For the most part we were inexperienced in the work and had to contend with financial stringency, which prevented our having many things which we now know to be needful; but from the beginning we set ourselves a clear ideal. Mount Olivet was to be not an 'institution' but a home.

How could this be accomplished with a collection of lads of an average of seventeen years, some of whom had never known home life, for it is a condition that can never be completely imitated. Some imitations are irritating.

If we were to avoid becoming institutional or an irritating and unreal imitation of a family home where there are only four or five members, we must find a different kind of life. Now a Monk loves his Monastery more than his home—not becauses it imitates his home, but because it stands for a certain life which is quite different. Obviously we could not make Monks out of all our boys, or expect them to lead a life resembling that of Religious; but could we build up the work and the boys' life around the Monastery rather than have an instit-

41

ution managed and staffed by Religious?

I think we may claim to have done so, and our success with the boys has been mainly due to this fact.

We have created an atmosphere for the work which is neither home nor institution. The thing that looms large is the life of the *Monastery*, and the frequent visits of priests who come because of the Community life, as well as the organised pilgrimages to the Shrine of Christ the King, impress the boys with the fact that the important thing is the Monastery, and that in so doing they are learning the things they need to know. The idea of being in an institution has faded from their minds.

A Comfortable Company devotes some of its pages to extracts from *The Frensham Gazette*, an internal house organ of which every boy regularly received a copy. There is mention, for instance, of a Shrove Tuesday party in St Vincent's House, with a good meal provided by Brother Ignatius and the kitchen staff.

The *Frensham Gazette* used to record, together with Brother Joseph's comments, particularly flagrant examples of bad behaviour on the part of boys. Mentally retarded juveniles are extremely unreliable, so it is no surprise to read of an outbreak of fire in the laundry. Two boys were tried by a Court of Honour, made up of other boys, and were found guilty of setting fire to the clothes and woodwork by interfering with the switches, and leaving the electric irons on. What penalty was imposed is not recorded. Brother Joseph says in *A Comfortable Company* that corporal punishment is unknown at Mount Olivet, and that any punishment needed takes the form of withdrawal of privileges. Some retarded boys have altogether exceptional appetites, and thefts of food from the larder were not uncommon. I remember an occasion when a boy, quite a small boy actually, ate two large loaves of bread at a sitting.

On another occasion Brother Joseph had just returned from London, and asked one of the senior and more reliable boys to drive his small, bright-red sports car, his pride and joy, into the garage for him as he was in a hurry. The boy drove it not only into the garage but out the other side, carrying away the garage's further wooden wall. This provoked considerable mirth among the bystanders, of whom I happened to be one; but our laughter had to be damped down as the Brother Superior was still within earshot. He would not have appreciated the humour of the situation.

In the first years at Mount Olivet there was no resident chaplain; visiting clergymen or monks from Nashdom supplied at weekends and on major festivals, as far as was possible. The first resident chaplain was the Reverend William Francis Wyber. It is not clear when he arrived; it would seem not until 1934. W.F. Wyber was ordained deacon in 1915 and priest in 1918, by the Bishop of Llandaff. His entry in *Crockford* makes no mention of any university or theological college. The three-year gap between his admission to deacon's and priest's orders is puzzling. From 1915 – 1921 he was assistant curate at Merthyr Tydfil; the same at Pontesbury from 1926 – 1931. There is another gap in his record between 1921 and 1926. What can he have been doing during this time? Perhaps he had trouble with his health. In 1932 he was licensed to officiate in the diocese of Guildford; but he may perhaps not have come to Frensham straight away. He remained in the diocese until 1936, from which year until 1940 he was chaplain at St John's Convent, Sandymount, Dublin. Then he vanishes again for a further two years. In 1943 and 1944 he was licensed to officiate in the diocese of Bath and Wells. Later he is found at 7 Millman Street, London, WC1, exercising a kind of honorary assistant curacy at St Alban's, Holborn. His last entry in *Crockford* is in 1937, so probably he was dead by 1948.

Father Wyber seems to have been a bit of a rolling stone, and to have been of a retiring, rather nervous disposition. After he had left Frensham he became something of a legend there. He seems to have been regarded with affection and esteem, and a number of amusing stories about him were current. One of his *obiter dicta*, spoken with something of a drawl when he was trying to make polite conversation with a stranger, was: 'We've been having a lot of weather recently, haven't we?'

Some useful information about the running of the Mount Olivet Institution is given in the final pages of Brother Joseph's *A Comfortable Company*. The Institution's Managers, the Servants of Christ the King, are assisted by a Supervisory Committee for the Mental Deficiency Work, the members of the Committee being:

A.E. Pearce, Esq. (Chairman)
Dr Edythe Lindsay
Miss C.M.C.P. Carlyon (Public Assistance Committee)
Lady Blacker
The Rev. Mother Superior, Ss.Tr.
The Sister Mary Elisabeth, Ss.Tr.
The Rev. Dom Martin Collett, OSB
Brig.-General Drake, CB
Lieut.-Col. Boyd, DSO

The Local Government Authorities make a grant for the mainten-
ance of every defective sent by them to the Institution, but the balance
sheet shows that to maintain the present system and standard an
additional sum of £500 a year is needed from voluntary subscriptions.

The community pays at present nearly £300 a year in rent, and
the owners of the property have suggested a scheme under which
the purchase of the property could be commenced with an initial
payment of £500 and yearly payment of little more than the present
rent. The total amount needed is only £5,500, and it would be a
great relief to the community not to have to pay rent. A 'Monastery
Purchase Fund' has been opened.

In 1933 and '34 respectively the community gained two exceptional recruits. To say this is no reflection on the earlier members,
who all seem to have been good men, though they may have lacked
the staying power needed for a successful and lasting religious
vocation. One may wonder, perhaps, if some of them might have
survived if they had had a properly trained religious as their superior
and novice-master. These two new members were Joseph Reginald
Bullen (in religion Brother Anthony) and Godfrey John Fuller
(Brother Anselm).

Joseph Bullen was born in 1907, the son of Harry Bullen, a farmer
owning land near Bungay, in Suffolk. After her husband's death
Mrs Bullen married the Reverend Mr Huddle, vicar of Hasketon,
near Woodbridge. At Hasketon, and in the Woodbridge area, Joe
Bullen even as a boy made his mark on the church life of the parish.
A nativity play given in the church, which he directed himself,
made a considerable impression, and was long remembered. After
leaving school he worked for a time for a photographer in Norwich,

where he attended the church of St John Timberhill. He took his religion seriously, and the vicar of this church became his spiritual director. It was probably this clergyman who pointed him towards the Servants of Christ the King. He was twenty-six when he decided to try his vocation at Mount Olivet Monastery. He was of medium height, well-built, mentally well-balanced and self-assured, yet modest and unassertive, with a highly developed sense of humour. With his good looks, ready smile, and pleasant manner he made a favourable impression; whatever he did was done with a quiet and willing thoroughness.

John Fuller (Brother Anselm), a tall, thin man of about the same age as Brother Anthony, came from Dover, where he had worked in his father's carpentry and joinery business. He was an Anglo-Catholic, and knew Father Baverstock. Perhaps he had met this well-known priest on some occasion when he was preaching in Dover. This meeting, wherever it took place, led to John Fuller's joining Father Baverstock at Hinton Martell, where he helped the Rector in various ways, but more especially in looking after the mentally defective boys who were living there under Father Baverstock's care. Father Baverstock and John Fuller were among those who encouraged Brother Joseph to take up work for mental defectives; a little later John left to join the community at Mount Olivet. Brother Anselm, as he was called in the community, was rather highly-strung, and was of a more nervous temperament than Brother Anthony, less able to take decisions; but he was a man of energy and good will, helpful, good-natured, not lacking in a sense of humour—always so desirable in a candidate for the religious life. He was a man likely to be an asset to any community that he might join; to Brother Joseph he must have seemed a real gift from heaven because of his abilities as a handyman, and his experience with mentally defective boys.

Brother Anthony replaced the expelled Brother Ignatius as cook to the community and Institution, a function that he fulfilled admirably. The Brothers and the boys ate together in a common refectory, with a high table at one end for the Brothers, the chaplain, and any guests who might be staying. Brother Joseph was a notably small eater, and sometimes got very impatient over the 'enormous quantities' of food that he accused the other Brothers, quite unjustly, of consuming. His own small appetite was probably a sign of his poor health.

Brother Anselm was the community's bursar, and kept the accounts of both the community and the Institution. In this responsible office he showed himself to be most capable; but he was allowed very little say in the actual administration of the finances, Brother Joseph himself being the sole decision-maker.

Brother Anthony and Brother Anselm soon became twin pillars of the enterprise at Mount Olivet; sadly, each of them lived to rue the day when he had 'signed on' under Brother Joseph's command.

A careful reader of Brother Joseph's *Christus Rex* article on 'Keeping the Laity in the Dark' would have surmised that in 1933 the community was suffering from a rather severe attack of 'Roman Fever'. Given the extreme papalist ethos prevailing at Mount Olivet, such attacks were inevitable from time to time; but so severe was this one that the Reverend Brother Superior actually sought an interview with the Roman Catholic Bishop of Southwark, Dr Peter Emmanuel Amigo, in order to discuss the matter with him. He was kindly received, but the interview led to no immediate result. After he had got home again, the patient's temperature seems to have gone down. On further reflection the community decided that they could not deny the validity of their past sacramental life within the Church of England. In a letter which he wrote to the Bishop two and a half years later Brother Joseph said that after the interview he had realized that if they had made their submission to Rome at that point 'only disaster, and possibly financial collapse' would have followed; which would not have been to the glory of God nor for the honour of the Church.

Things seem to have settled down again quite quickly, and during 1934 went on much as usual; but the fundamental problems, both spiritual and temporal, still remained. The General Report submitted by Brother Joseph to the Institution's Committee of Management in May 1935 speaks of 'far-reaching decisions' that have had to be made. There seems to have been some kind of upheaval in the community—probably the departure of some of the Brothers—and one of the decisions made was that 'the Community must be composed only of men who could take a responsible share in the management of the Institution and the training of boys; so that there is no room for young men and youths who need a good deal of training and oversight themselves'. Some people might have thought that Brother Joseph himself stood in need of a good deal of training and oversight; but it was too late to think of that now. A point had been reached at which the Institution was claiming and receiving more of the Brother Superior's attention than did his community. Dr Waller Todd's statement in his Introduction to *A Comfortable Company*, 'So the Monastery still comes first', was no longer true, except as a matter of theory.

The same Report to the Committee of Management says that the decision taken in respect of recruits to the community has meant a reduction in the community's numbers—which presumably were small enough already—but that it has improved the character of the work of the Institution by ensuring that all buying, ordering, and economies are in the hands of responsible people. During the past year the expenditure has been reduced by over £1,000. On the other hand, 'We have never recovered financially from the expenses of opening the Institution and the delay of several months before patients were received.' This is borne out by the testimony of Mr Hall (Brother Martin), who was there until 1935, when he left to take up training for the teaching profession. Mr Hall says, 'Anything and everything that could go wrong when we arrived at Frensham did so, and it was the delay in opening the house for the reception of mentally handicapped boys that almost brought the Community to an end. The Mother Superior and the Sisters of the Transfiguration at Basingstoke saved the day with a financial gift and grant.'

Perhaps something should now be said about the religious observance at Mount Olivet. Among the illustrations in *A Comfortable Company* is a small photograph of the sanctuary in the temporary chapel set up by the Brothers when they arrived. The altar appears to be a simple wooden table, with the customary white altar-cloths, but no frontal. There is a square, quite small, veiled tabernacle, set into a gradine behind the altar, and on the gradine are the six candlesticks, again quite small, customary in the Roman rite. Placed on pedestals near the altar are statues, of the painted-plaster, commercial kind, of the Sacred Heart and the Blessed Virgin.

The permanent chapel inaugurated a little later was much more impressive. No photographs of it have survived, but in *Christus Rex* for Michaelmas 1937 there is a whole-page drawing of the altar by Brother Joseph's artist-friend and supporter, Mr Marshall Barnes. The altar is in the baroque style; that is to say, its front of painted wood is surrounded by an ornate, scroll-like frame of gilded wood; which is how I remember it. There is no gradine, but fixed to the back of the *mensa* is a large domed tabernacle, completely covered by a silk *conopaeum* or veil. On either side of the tabernacle are three rather tall gilt candlesticks, holding tall candles. The space between the altar and the wall behind it is filled with an arras or hanging which, if I remember rightly, was bright red. To the left of the altar, suspended from a bracket in the wall, is an ornate baroque sanctuary lamp. On the walls to right and left of the altar are pictures of saints, in gilt frames. The space between the communion rails and the altar is quite narrow, so liturgical functions, such as High Mass, must have been a little difficult to carry out.

By 1935, if not earlier, the daily Mass was said in Latin, from the *Missale Romanum*. Earlier, Knott and Company's *The English Missal*—basically the Roman Missal in the vernacular—had been in use; but when one day Brother Joseph consulted the chaplain about the possibility of changing from English to Latin, Father Wyber had replied: 'Well, the Romans have the Latin [pronounced 'Lahtin'], don't they? So I suppose *we* can.' And the change was made. The boys seem to have accepted it uncomplainingly. Perhaps it was all Greek to them; but they were content to be guided by Brother Joseph in such matters. In any case, the understanding of sacred rites is not dependent on a knowledge of the language in which they are conducted. Ritualism has its own language, the language of symbolism and poetry. But even in 1935 it was an immemorial custom in English Catholic churches that the chief instructional parts of the Mass, the Lesson (or Epistle) and Gospel, should be read in the mother-tongue.

The predominant colour-scheme in the chapel was Brother Joseph's

A poster for the Circus

More House School

favourite red and gold. His famous preaching cross—destined, alas, to perish in the fire of 1972—stood in a corner of the sacristy, and did occasional duty as a processional cross. From the Art and Book Company he had acquired a complete set, in the different liturgical colours, of Spanish eucharistic vestments of a singularly graceful cut—very different from the usual 'fiddleback' Roman chasuble. These vestments matched perfectly with Brother Joseph's baroque *ensemble*. In such matters he had excellent taste. He must have spent a lot of money on fitting up this chapel, just as he did on the purchase of handsome pieces of antique furniture for the house; supposedly with the intention of impressing the parents, or prospective parents, of boys. In respect of the chapel he certainly acted on the Huysmanesque principle of *le luxe pour Dieu*. Brother Anselm and Brother Anthony sometimes inclined to be a little doubtful about this; but Brother Joseph could have evoked, had he been aware of it—perhaps he was?—St Thomas Aquinas's dictum that 'It belongs to the virtue of Magnificence to spend largely in pursuit of noble objects.'

The peak years of the SCK's popularity in the Anglo-Catholic world were 1933 – 36. Brother Joseph's gifts as a preacher had done much to make the community known, and as its reputation rose, so there rose with it Brother Joseph's personal estimation of his status as a Religious Founder and Superior. This was to reach unprecedented heights, which today seem hardly credible. However, self-instructed and self-guided as he was, he should perhaps not be criticized too severely, bearing in mind the high esteem in which he held monastic authority.

At the Abbey House at Pershore he had taken to wearing a black skull-cap, pectoral cross, and buckled shoes. At Frensham he went further. When he attended choir with the Brothers—and his many affairs saw to it that his attendance was not always as regular as it might have been—the Brothers had to enter the chapel and take their places first. Only then did the Reverend Brother Superior make his own impressive entrance, wearing over his habit a rochet with a deep fringe of lace, together with his pectoral cross and *zuchetto*. When making this grand entrance he was preceded by two of the more reliable boys, vested as acolytes in cassock and cotta, and bearing lighted tapers. In this abbatial style he was conducted to the Superior's place, and Divine Service could then begin.

However, some time after the community's move to Frensham all attempt at reciting in common any kind of formal Office was abandoned—perhaps because of fewness of numbers, perhaps because the demands of the Institution left little time for liturgical devotions—and five daily decades of the Rosary, said in common, were substituted. The Brothers now took to wearing, after the fashion of Dominicans, large chaplets of black rosary beads, suspended from their girdles. All this was highly unBenedictine, to say the least. Following on this marked simplification in the Community's liturgical life, Brother Joseph gave up his state entrance into the chapel; and his rochet—a vestment peculiar to bishops, abbots, protonotaries apostolic *ad instar participantium*, and a few other prelates—was cast aside. But he was careful to retain his pectoral cross, which he regarded as the essential outward symbol of his rank as Superior of a religious community. For the same reason he continued to prefix an episcopal † to his signature.

Late in 1935 he succumbed to another attack of Roman Fever, the most severe yet, leading, it would seem, almost to a state of delirium in which he virtually expelled himself from the Church of England. There was nothing left for him to do but once again approach the Latin-rite Bishop of Southwark, Dr Amigo. In a preliminary letter to the Bishop he affirmed that 'Neither the difficulties on the spiritual and material side now exist, and I desire to ask your lordship to receive Brother Anthony, Brother Anselm, and myself into the Catholic Church.'

The disordered syntax of this sentence perhaps reflects the Reverend Brother's agitation of mind. Even if the SCK's financial position had somewhat improved, he was badly mistaken if he thought that the proposed change of spiritual allegiance would not now entail serious financial consequences. But he was really in no position to take this into account. The fact was that the community's petition for reconciliation with the Holy See had been precipitated by a wholly unforeseen cataclysmic event, which had taken place in the early autumn.

The occasion was a big pilgrimage to Mount Olivet Monastery

from some of those London churches whose clergy and people enjoyed these pious excursions to the Shrine of Christ the King. For these gatherings the statue from the shrine on the loggia was moved to an outdoor site at the bottom of the garden. This special pilgrimage shrine was a modest affair, comprising little more than a pedestal for the statue, with a covering above it, and a temporary altar in front. (In later years this shrine was enclosed with wire meshing, and served as an aviary for exotic birds, imported from Asian parts: a sad secularization in the eyes of any who remembered the days of hope and promise.)

Picture the scene. On this autumn day in 1935 two or three hundred pilgrims, men and women, stood on the terraced slopes overlooking the outdoor shrine. The Mass had begun; the deacon had sung the Gospel, and the celebrant, Dom Martin Collett, now Abbot of Nashdom, wearing his mitre, had taken his seat, flanked by his deacon and subdeacon, two monks of his community. At this point Brother Joseph, who had appointed himself preacher for the occasion, stepped forward and knelt for the Abbot's blessing. He then started his sermon, which began conventionally enough, with introductory sentiments and reflections appropriate to the occasion. But suddenly something seemed to snap in the preacher's brain, just as on the occasion of the outdoor sermon at Staithes six years previously. To the astonishment of his hearers, Brother Joseph turned towards the Abbot and his assistant clergy and launched into a tirade which denounced the Anglo-Catholic movement in the English Church as a fraud and a sham. The whole thing, he declared, was an act of make-belief.

As soon as Brother Joseph realized what he had said he fled the scene. Overcome by the enormity of what he had done he took refuge in the monastery kitchen, overwhelmed by the full horror of the situation in which he had so publicly placed himself by his thoughtless words. And there he remained until the last of the pilgrims had gone.

Clearly there was now nothing for it, if the community were not to founder totally, but to go the whole way and seek reconciliation with Rome.

It is doubtful if this is what Brother Joseph, in his calmer moments, really wanted. In all probability he would have taken this step eventually, but at a time of his own choosing: a time when his community should have built up its strength—it was now at a low ebb, with a membership of only three—and have become more firmly established. It is doubtful, too, if his companions were quite ready for such a step. Brother Anthony perhaps was; Brother Anselm fairly certainly was not. But out of loyalty to Brother Joseph and to the community both agreed to commit themselves. So a new approach was made to the Bishop of Southwark, who was told by Brother Joseph that he and his companions were now longing to be under the rule of a bishop 'who holds the same faith as ourselves'. Had Brother Joseph known a little more about the Right Reverend Peter Emmanuel Amigo, a notoriously formidable prelate, he might not have been quite so delighted at the prospect of coming under his rule; but in the event he was lucky, for Dr Amigo was to treat him with quite exceptional indulgence: a testimony to the Founder-Superior's charm and his powers of persuasion.

Dr Amigo was a good pastoral bishop, with a great love of the poor; but he did not much care for religious orders. In 1910 he had placed the priory of the Premonstratensian Canons at Storrington under an interdict, which lasted until the Bishop's death some forty years later; and in the early 1920s it was he who had played a prominent part in bringing to nought the saintly Father Benedict Williamson's attempt to re-found the male branch of the Bridgettine Order. Such being the Bishop's general attitude to religious orders, it is surprising that he did not insist on the dissolution of Brother Joseph's minuscule community there and then before they made their individual acts of submission to the Holy See. Why did he not do so? Most probably because this would have threatened the continued existence of the Institution for which the Brothers were responsible. It seems that the Bishop considered that his diocese was more or less completely furnished with every kind of good work, with the one exception of a Home for mentally retarded boys. With the reception into the Church of the Servants of Christ the King this deficiency would be made good without the slightest effort on the part of the diocese. In fact, Brother Anthony used always to maintain that this was the sole reason for the Bishop's remarkable benevolence in allowing the little community to remain in being.

So one day towards the end of January 1936 Brother Joseph, wearing his grey habit and the big leather gauntlets that he affected when driving his red sports car, drove through the Surrey lanes to the main road to London, on his way to Bishop's House, St George's Road, SE1, there to learn from the Bishop what destiny was intended for himself and his companions. When the time came, he was relieved to hear that the Bishop wished the Community to continue its corporate existence, but to be affiliated to some established religious order, to which it could look for guidance. What Order would Brother Joseph and his confrères choose? Brother Joseph, who had by no means forgotten his early devotion to St Dominic, suggested that perhaps the Servants of Christ the King might be reconstituted as a community of Dominican Third Order Brothers. This was an unhappy choice, because of all religious Orders the Dominicans were the one Dr Amigo could least abide.

Remarking that there was no house of Dominican friars in the diocese, the Bishop suggested that instead they should become Franciscan Tertiary Brothers. On the face of it, this was a very good idea, for the principal work of the Brothers, the care of mentally defective boys, was eminently Franciscan in character. Had this suggestion been accepted the community could have been placed under the direction of the Friars Minor at their novitiate house at Chilworth, Surrey, not far from Frensham. But now it was Brother Joseph's turn to demur, and he respectfully but firmly explained, in so many words, that he could not stand Franciscans at any price.

Very likely the Bishop felt much the same. At any rate, in the end it was decided that the Servants of Christ the King should remain Benedictine oblate brothers, under the direction of the only house of Black Monks in the Southwark diocese, St Augustine's Abbey, Ramsgate.

But really this was not a good solution; if only because Ramsgate, though undoubtedly in the diocese of Southwark, was just about as far from Frensham as it was possible to be. By contrast, only a few miles from Frensham was Farnborough Abbey, a Benedictine house of the Solesmes Congregation. If the Farnborough monks had been willing to accept responsibility for the little community at Frensham things might have turned out very differently. But Farnborough was in the diocese of Portsmouth, and it would have been against Dr Amigo's principles to allow any religious institute under his own jurisdiction to be linked, however tenuously, with another diocese.

So the decision was made in favour of Ramsgate. But since the Ramsgate monks were not a large community, and already had the care of a school, and the administration of several parishes in the Isle of Thanet, perhaps they were not overjoyed at having this new charge, which they could hardly decline, thrust upon them. Nor, perhaps, was the Abbot of Ramsgate, the Right Reverend Dom Adrian Taylor, the happiest of choices as the SCK's new higher superior, to which office the Bishop delegated him.

Before they could be reconciled with the Holy See the three Brothers had to receive a course of instruction, so as to make sure that they really knew, understood, and subscribed to all the doctrines of the Roman Catholic Church. True, all three men had held virtually the totality of these doctrines for years; but still, in so grave a matter it is always necessary to make assurance doubly sure. The question of who was to take charge of the Brothers' instruction was of particular interest to the Roman Catholic priest in Farnham, within the bounds of whose parish Frensham lay. The man in question was the Reverend Etienne Robo, a shrewd, hard-headed Breton. Brother Joseph was fated never really to get on with Father Robo, who was irritated right at the beginning of their relationship when he received from Father Anthony Lowe, a Dominican friend of Brother Joseph's, a letter suggesting that he, Father Lowe, might be allowed to undertake the Brothers' instruction. Father Lowe, who claimed to be, and possibly was, the last of the Plantagenets, had spent most of his priestly life in the British West Indies. In 1930 ill-health had forced him to return to England, and by 1935 he was something of an invalid. His interest in the Servants of Christ the King did him credit; but even Brother Joseph came to see that he was not quite the right man for the delicate task for which he had proposed himself. So Father Robo must have been relieved when he learned that the Brothers' instruction was to be undertaken by Monsignor Philip Hallett, the Rector of St John's Seminary, near Guildford.

While this matter was still under consideration, Father Robo, on 18 January 1936, wrote a letter to Canon Serafin Banfi, one of the Bishop's Vicars-General, in which he said:

> Brother Joseph is certainly very much in earnest; he knows, no doubt, some theology in patches, such as one learns without a master—but: for many years he has been in rebellion against his own parish clergyman and against his bishop, and he has to learn the ways of obedience, both as a moral discipline and as a practical necessity of everyday life . . . The house is merely rented. There are debts. The income does not cover the expenditure. I reckon Brother Joseph will have to find yearly from £1,000 to £1,5000 by begging appeals to cover normal expenditure. In a word, he will need the assistance of the Catholic public.

This was a thoroughly realistic assessment. If the Bishop saw this letter, and presumably he did, it is a very great pity that he did not pay more attention to it.

In March, on the Tuesday in Holy Week, the three Brothers were received into the Catholic and Roman Church at a simple ceremony conducted by Monsignor Hallett in the chapel at Mount Olivet. For Brother Joseph this joyful occasion held also a tinge of sadness. He had well and truly burned his boats, more by accident than design, and was leaving behind him a multitude of friends and supporters from whom he would hear no more; and he was entering an unknown territory which he may have suspected, in his more thoughtful moments, to be full of hazards.

In the Church of England he had enjoyed considerable status as the founder and superior of one of that Church's relatively few religious communities of men; but even sympathetic Roman Catholics, familiar as they were with the ancient orders of monks, canons, friars, and the more modern congregations of clerks regular, were not likely to be greatly interested in so small and obscure a fraternity as the Servants of Christ the King. This was doubly so because in those days, fifty years ago, orders and congregations of Brothers were by no means so highly regarded as were the various clerical orders. The members of these lay fraternities—Alexian and Xaverian Brothers, Brothers of St John of God, Brothers of the Christian Schools, Presentation Brothers, and so on—bore this very humbly. Often on their lips, when they were mistaken for priests, were the words: 'Oh, but I am only a Brother.' It was with this category of religious that the SCK would be identified in the general Roman Catholic mind.

Brother Joseph probably did not fully realize this; but he seemed all too keenly aware of what was happening when, on the occasion of his abjuration of schism and heresy, he had to surrender his pectoral cross, the ultimate symbol in his own and other Anglican eyes of his special status. In later years Brother Anthony used to say that it was evident to him that at the moment of the handing over of his pectoral cross something in Brother Joseph's heart died completely and for ever. He believed that Brother Joseph never fully recovered from this blow, which had its effect upon his subsequent life and conduct.

However, one need not doubt that this memorable day was essentially a joyful one for the three Brothers, who after years of hesitations and uncertainties now found themselves with their feet firmly planted on the Rock of Peter.

They had wondered, naturally, how the Board of Control and the parents of the boys under their care would react to the community's change of religious allegiance. Would the parents perhaps decide to remove their sons? In the event, none did so, and the Board of Control made no difficulties. The parents seem mostly not to have held any very definite religious views. They had great confidence in Brother Joseph, and were content to leave such matters to him. After the change the boys will have noticed little or no difference in the religious instruction they received, nor in the way the chapel services were conducted.

The Servants of Christ the King were now a 'diocesan institute', approved *ad experimentum* by the Bishop of Southwark, and subject to his jurisdiction. Only after a number of years had gone by, and then only if the community had acquired enough members to establish another house, could application be made for approval by the Holy See. If this were granted, the community would then pass from the Bishop's jurisdiction to that of the Sacred Congregation for Religious, in Rome.

For the time being Abbot Taylor was to act as their higher superior, in virtue of the authority delegated to him by the Bishop. As was hinted earlier, this was not to prove a very happy arrangement. No doubt Abbot Taylor possessed some of the qualities which St Benedict desiderates in an abbot; but if so, they did not exactly shine out in his dealings with Frensham. No doubt he had his merits. Certainly he was a brave man, for when serving as an Army chaplain in the war of 1914-18 he had been awarded the Military Cross.

The three Brothers now began their novitiate: a year of testing and training in the religious life, in accordance with the spirit of St Benedict's Holy Rule, and in accordance with new Constitutions approved for the SCK by the Bishop. Father Wyber, not having seen his way to abjure communion with the primatial See of Canterbury, had left the scene; sorrowfully, we may be sure. He was not young, and having to renew his wandering life, from this obscure and poorly paid appointment to that, must have been hard for him.

As the new chaplain, and also as the community's immediate superior and novice-master, the Abbot had appointed one of his own monks, Dom Bede Winslow. But as Brother Joseph explained in *Christus Rex* for Michaelmas 1937, just as their novitiate year was coming to an end: 'The position here has been complicated by reason of the active work undertaken by the Community, and it has been necessary for Brother Joseph to continue to act as superior in the house and the management of the work in order that it should be effectively carried on; but Dom Bede Winslow has acted as novice-master and represented the higher superior, the Abbot of Ramsgate.' The implication that may be drawn from this candid avowal is that Dom Bede was never really able to function as superior at all. The deduction would be approximately correct. The instructions which Dom Bede gave as novice-master were most valuable; but his authority in the place was severely restricted; far more than it should have been. For this the fault must lie with Abbot Taylor, who ought to have realized that someone less 'gentlemanly' than Father Bede was needed as superior if anything were to be made of Brother Joseph as a religious.

Dom Bede Winslow was a devout and scholarly monk, no weakling, but of unfailing courtesy and consideration; he really was not made to cope with such a one as Reginald Joseph Gard'ner. There was, however, one matter in which he did succeed in obtaining Brother Joseph's compliance with his wishes; a minor matter, indeed, but one which it must have cost Brother Joseph a good deal to comply with. Dom Bede had managed to get the Brothers' habit redesigned, on what he considered a more monastic pattern; that had presented no great difficulty. His real triumph was over the black cord which Dom Martin Collett had had substituted for the original bright red girdle. But Dom Bede regarded all cord girdles, of whatever colour—except for the white triple-knotted cord of the Friars Minor—as 'Anglican'. (Perhaps he had in mind the black cord of the Cowley Fathers.) Over this matter he was uncharacteristically firm, and the SCK's cord was replaced by the customary monastic belt of black leather.

Monastic hospitality was not much in evidence at Mount Olivet, I suppose because of the unusual nature of the monastery. However, in 1937 a not infrequent visitor was Dr Sergius Bolshakoff, a Russian émigré who had acquired his doctorate in philosophy at Oxford. Presumably the attraction for him was the presence of Dom Bede Winslow, who happened to be the founder and editor of *The Eastern Churches Quarterly*. Dr Bolshakoff was a great worker for the cause of reunion of the Eastern and Western Churches, and was the author of a number of valuable books, including *The Christian Church and the Soviet State* (1941) and *I Mistici Russi* (1962). The latter work was published in English as *The Russian Mystics*, with a preface by Thomas Merton, in 1976.

The Brothers' novitiate, more nominal than real, was now over. Of course, ideally they should have been sent to some monastery or monasteries of strict observance for their year of training and probation; circumstances at Mount Olivet had made that impossible. So on the last Sunday of October 1937, the Feast of the Kingship

of our Lord Jesus Christ, the three Brothers made their vows—
'temporary' vows, binding for the next three years only— into the
hands of Abbot Taylor, who then formally installed, or reinstalled,
Brother Joseph as superior (and novice-master). Seeing that he had
already held these posts, of his own appointment, for ten years, it
might have been thought that it was time for a change. Had this
change been made he could still have retained his position as Principal of the Institution, for which he was by now qualified in the
school of experience. But as far as the community was concerned,
if Abbot Taylor had taken a closer interest in it he would have
realized that Brother Anthony was of a more stable and prudent
personality than Brother Joseph, capable of taking charge of the
community's destiny for a period; and that such a change would
be to the community's advantage.

Father Bede, who among other things had taught the Brothers
to recite in choir the Day Hours of the Church, from the *Diurnum
Monasticum*, now returned to his monastery. Having no one avail-
able to replace him, Abbot Taylor applied to Prinknash Abbey,
another monastery of the Cassinese Congregation of the Primitive
Observance, to which Ramsgate Abbey belonged. Happily, the
Abbot of Prinknash was able to send to Frensham as chaplain an
elderly monk of American origin, Dom Ambrose Holly, a man of
attractive personality and much spiritual wisdom.

Earlier in his life Dom Ambrose, then the Reverend Norman
Holly, had been the Catholic priest in Pershore. There he had set
up in Priest Lane a 'tin tabernacle', painted outside in dark green,
which served the papists of Pershore as their place of worship down
to its replacement in 1959 by the present more stylish brick church
of the Holy Redeemer, St Wulfstan, and St Eadburga, a rather cold
and unwelcoming building, though correct in all the more recent
liturgical appointments. One can be quite sure that under Father
Holly's care the tin tabernacle was a charming and devotional place
of worship, however humble; it is sadly nostalgic to find it still
standing today, though somewhat forlornly, in a builder's yard
down the road, where it has been adapted to secular uses.

After the combined euphoria and *Angst* of the conversion of the
SCK Brothers, things at first seemed to go on well enough; but

Brother Joseph's editorial in *Christus Rex* for Lady Day 1937 sounds a warning note when it says that as a consequence of the conversion 'we have lost over two thousand supporters'. In the next number, for Michaelmas, the Community Notes say that 'Until we have more Brothers we cannot attempt any other kind of activity, and indeed we badly need more to help us maintain our present work for mentally defective boys. This, however, does not mean that those who have no particular aptitude for immediate contact with the boys would be obliged to do so. There are many departments of the work which contribute to its general success, but which are not immediately connected with the boys under our care.' This was a complete reversal of the former policy of recruiting only young men with an aptitude for such work.

In the same number of the magazine it is announced that the Servants of Christ the King have been asked to take over the promotion within the British Isles of the Church Unity Octave.

This annual week of prayer for Christian Unity had been instituted in 1908 by Paul James Francis Wattson, an American Episcopalian clergyman who in 1898 had founded the Society of the Atonement, Franciscans of the Third Order Regular, with a feminine branch led by Sister Lurana (Lurana Mary White). In 1909 the Atonement fathers, brothers, and sisters, fifteen in number, had been received corporately into the Roman Catholic Church. The Church Unity Octave week of prayer took place each year, beginning on 18 January, the feast of St Peter's Chair at Rome, and ending on 25 January, the feast of the Conversion of St. Paul. It had received the approval of successive popes, and its promotion was a most suitable work for the SCK. In England the Octave was observed somewhat patchily by Roman Catholics, depending on the enthusiasm or lack of it of the parish priests. The Frensham Brothers now took on the work of arranging preachers for the larger special services held throughout the country, looking after the distribution of posters, prayer leaflets, and so on. Brother Joseph welcomed warmly this new apostolate; but he must surely have felt it keenly that he himself was not to be one of the special preachers; in the 1930s the pulpit in Roman Catholic churches was still strictly a clerical monopoly.

of August. Training had continued all through the previous winter. The *Farnham Herald* of 2 January had printed a photograph of a Sumatra pony, 'formerly with the Royal Italian Circus', being put through its paces for three performances in the Frensham Village Institute during the coming week. On 13 February a performance in the Drill Hall at Aldershot had taken place before an audience of six hundred. On 22 May the *Herald* reported that over one thousand people had attended the Circus at Mount Olivet during the past week, beginning on the previous Friday, with performances every week-night up to Wednesday, and with matinées on Saturday and Monday.

Unhappily, however, the brilliant success of the Frensham Circus was to be a principal factor in the disintegration and dissolution of the Servants of Christ the King.

Brother Joseph's energy and stamina were astonishing; but he was physically frail, and such a punishing schedule could only weaken his health further, as well as straining his nerves to the uttermost. Also, it left him with little or no time and energy with which to fulfil his rôle as the superior of a religious community. The truth of the matter was that although Reginald Gard'ner, alias Rex Lynn Linton, had managed to transform himself into the Reverend Brother Joseph, SCK, he still remained at heart, and in essence, an actor and a showman. The histrionic element in his personality had remained deeply engrained in him, and by 1936 it could be repressed no longer.

And there were other troubles; firstly the urgent and ever-present problem of finance. And then there was his capacity for making enemies (as well as friends); or, to put it more mildly, the difficulty he had in getting on with his neighbours; among whom must be counted Father Robo and a certain Mr Warren, who lived near Mount Olivet and was a friend of Dom Bede Winslow's. For a time I was allowed to coach one of Mr Warren's sons in Latin for some public examination: the Common Entrance, perhaps; but after Mr Warren and Brother Joseph had fallen out my visits to the Warrens' house, which I much enjoyed, had to cease. Things even went so far that Brother Joseph inhibited Mr Warren from attending Mass in the Mount Olivet chapel. Mr Warren went to

Bishop's House, Southwark, to appeal in person, but the Bishop ruled against him.

The monastery chapel had been licensed by the Bishop as a semi-public oratory, which meant that the few Catholics who lived in Frensham could attend Mass there on Sundays, instead of travelling the three miles to St Joan of Arc's, Farnham. Mount Olivet's thirty boys filled most of the chapel, but there were five or six chairs at the back reserved for these local worshippers. Father Robo was never happy with this arrangement, but there was nothing he could do about it. It was just another factor in the rather strained relations that existed between himself, as parish priest, and the superior of Mount Olivet.

The chapel was, in fact, destined to exacerbate the mutual suspicion that existed between these two men. Knowing Father Robo's feelings about the chapel, Brother Joseph insisted that the Brother Sacristan should be very careful to see to it on Sunday mornings that only the five or six regular worshippers from outside were admitted. If any others presented themselves he was discreetly to ascertain whence they came and why, and to explain to them the delicacy of the situation. Imagine, therefore, the consternation of the sacristan, Brother Edmund, when on a Sunday morning in the summer of 1937 he saw outside the chapel's still unlocked french windows quite a little crowd, certainly no less than ten, of unknown women standing in the garden and banging on the glass door for admission.

With considerable misgiving the Brother turned the key and unlocked the door. Standing on the step, he began to try to explain to them why they could not fulfil their Sunday Mass obligation in Mount Olivet chapel, but must repair to their parish church. The Brother was quite a small man, of delicate build, and the next thing he knew was that he had been swept aside; the women surged into the chapel, where they immediately occupied all the chairs set out for the regular visitors, so that more had to be fetched from the refectory. When Brother Joseph arrived on the scene he was much displeased, and the situation grew very tense as he explained to the women, in forcible terms and tones, the irregularity and enormity of their action.

No progress being made, Dom Bede Winslow was then summoned from the sacristy to try to make some sense of things; but the ladies were all quite clear on one point: unless they were allowed to attend the Mass about to be celebrated, Father Bede would be responsible for their missing Mass altogether; for on no account would they enter the doors of St Joan of Arc's, Farnham. So they were allowed to stay, and to give their explanations afterwards, which they did in the Mount Olivet entrance hall, where a very odd story emerged.

At St Joan of Arc's on the previous Sunday Father Robo had told his congregations that in his opinion there was really only one thing still wanting before the parish could be considered complete and developed in every detail. What was still lacking was a sodality of the Children of Mary.

The Children of Mary was a pious association of girls and young women which in those days was established in nearly all Catholic parish churches and convent chapels. Its purpose was the fostering of devotion to the Mother of our Saviour, and a principal public rôle of the members was to carry, on its feretory, the statue of our Lady, and to walk behind it in a body, in the processions held on her greater festivals, especially during the months of May and October. When taking part in these pious exercises the Children of Mary wore white veils and blue mantles, producing an effect that was intended to be at once edifying and picturesque.

All of this Father Robo carefully explained to his flock, telling them that at seven o'clock on the following Thursday evening there would be a preliminary meeting in the Presbytery to discuss the feasibility of establishing the Children of Mary in St Joan's parish. All young women and girls who might be interested were invited to attend.

When Thursday evening came, and Father Robo went to the room where the aspirant Children of Mary were to assemble, he stood in the doorway aghast. For in front of him he saw ten or more women not one of whom could by any stretch of the imagination have been described as 'young', still less as a 'girl'. The good pastor's reaction was not discreet. Turning on his heel he swiftly left the room; but as he did so he could be heard muttering, with

65

typical Breton bluntness: 'But you are all old, old! Go away, you are old!'

One can imagine the indignant consternation that ensued, the ruffling of middle-aged and elderly feathers. 'Well, really! I mean to say!' The affronted women hurriedly left the presbytery, vowing never again to set foot in their parish church, or to have any further dealings with its incumbent. It was this resolution to boycott St Joan's that was the cause of their presence at Mount Olivet on the following Sunday morning.

How it was all resolved—for such *contretemps* usually are resolved, eventually—I have no idea; but it certainly gave Father Robo reason to view the Frensham establishment with even less than the little favour he had previously accorded it; nor did it inspire any warmer feelings between the Reverend Brother Superior and his parish priest.

More serious, though, were Brother Joseph's difficulties with some of the tradespeople of Farnham, to whom money was owing. It became the harassed Brother Superior's tactic, when confronted with importunate creditors, to use Brother Anselm, the community's bursar, as a shield, telling them that it was no use their addressing themselves to himself, for such things did not belong to his department. They must apply to the Bursar. This placed Brother Anselm in an impossible position, and he became a very worried man. Brother Anthony felt no less concern; by now they both felt that the Circus had become a danger to the religious life of the community. Their attempts to convince Brother Joseph that things were getting out of hand, and that it was high time that steps were taken to right them, had only the effect of making him feel that he had lost the confidence of the two men in whom he had put all his trust, and that he was beginning to lose control.

In September 1938 a point came when Brother Joseph seemed on the verge of giving up the struggle. He retired to his room, and stayed there, coming neither to choir nor to meals. For some days he was not seen in the house at all, and he made no attempt to communicate with the Brothers. His meals were taken up to him by one of the boys. He was not thought to be ill, at least not in any serious way, and he did not ask for a doctor. Pretty certainly

66

he was in a state of acute depression, overwhelmed by his financial and other problems. An ominous silence seemed to overhang the house, and the Brothers, two professed and one novice, became increasingly anxious. Clearly something would soon have to be done. But what?

One might wonder that the chaplain was not appealed to, but I believe he was away at the time. The chaplain was then Dom Urban Rouvière, a monk of Ramsgate. He was either French or Belgian, and had been for some time chaplain to the Canonesses of St Augustine at Westgate-on-Sea. He was a gentle, elderly man, mildly eccentric in his ways. (Once when I knelt down in his room to make my confession to him he said, in his heavily accented English, 'For what we are about to receive may the Lord make us truly thankful', a formula usually employed as a grace before meals.) In any case, I doubt if Dom Urban could have made much headway with Brother Joseph; but he might perhaps have been able to give Brother Anthony and Brother Anselm some helpful advice.

Brother Anselm was particularly upset, for to all appearances the Reverend Brother Superior had retired from life, leaving no one in charge, even temporarily. There were decisions that needed to be made, but there was no one with the authority to make them. And there were always the creditors ... In desperation Brother Anselm made up his mind to write to the higher superior, the Abbot of Ramsgate, and ask him to make a canonical visitation of the house in order to find some way of resolving the impasse and straightening things out. In accordance with the canon law then in force—Cardinal Gasparri's *Codex Iuris Canonici*, published by the Vatican in 1917—the Constitutions of all religious orders and congregations reserved to local superiors the right to inspect all incoming and outgoing correspondence. The right was exercised sparingly. Outgoing letters were handed to the superior unsealed, but they were rarely examined. Incoming letters were normally distributed unopened. Novice-masters and -mistresses had the same rights of inspection; with incoming letters for novices they were usually content just to make a formal nick on the back of the envelope, which they left unopened. But a letter from a religious to his or her higher superior was exempt from scrutiny; the writer could seal the envelope, stamp it, and post it without reference to the local superior. This is what Brother Anselm had every right to do, and what he should have done: as Brother Anthony told him when Anselm sought his advice. But at the last moment Brother Anselm developed scruples of conscience, and could not bring himself to seal and post his letter to the Abbot. Instead, he went to Brother Joseph, who was in his room and in bed, told him what he was doing and why, and handed him the letter in its open, unstamped envelope. Brother Joseph glanced quickly through it, and then bade Brother Anselm leave the room, saying that he would deal with the matter. Moments later the Reverend Brother Superior was seen emerging from his room, fully clad, and carrying a small suitcase. Dashing down the stairs, he was instantly out of the house and away in his bright red sports car. There could be no doubt as to where he was going. A day later he reappeared, accompanied by the Right Reverend Dom Adrian Taylor. Brother Joseph then announced that the Abbot would interview all members of the community, one by one, in the library.

Abbot Taylor was not the most prepossessing of men, and an interview with him could be something of an ordeal. He had been wounded in the throat during the first world war, and spoke in a kind of loud, husky whisper, which could be disconcerting. What he had to say to Brother Anthony, Brother Anselm, and myself, the sole novice, was simple. Brother Joseph had said that he could no longer continue as superior. There was no one at Ramsgate who could be spared to replace him. Therefore the Congregation of the Servants of Christ the King would be canonically suppressed. Everyone except Brother Joseph must leave the house within the next few days. When Brother Anthony, the most courteous of men, commented on the extraordinary suddenness of this decision, the Abbot's only response was: 'I will hear nothing against Brother Joseph.'

Abbot Taylor had been requested by a professed religious, Brother Anselm, to make a canonical visitation of Mount Olivet Monastery, and to inquire into the difficulties prevailing there, with a view to finding a solution or solutions to the current grave problems. This he did not do. Instead, having heard only Brother Joseph's side of the story, he decided to act *motu proprio*; of course with the approval of the Bishop of Southwark.

The Abbot's manner when interviewing the Brothers was unsympathetic. The two professed Brothers were told that dispensations from their vows would be applied for, and that when the dispensations came through all they would have to do would be to append their signatures. Brother Anthony informed the Abbot that neither he nor Brother Anselm would willingly sign the papers since they had no wish to be relieved of their vows, and had not asked to have them dispensed. The Abbot then said that it would make no difference whether they signed the papers or not. To which Brother Anthony rejoined, not without some justification, that if that was how vows were regarded in the Roman Church, they were hardly worth taking seriously at all.

I think that by the end of these interviews we all knew exactly how the English monks and friars of the sixteenth century felt when they were turned out of their monasteries by the agents of King Henry VIII. However, once Brother Joseph had made up his mind to resign, the decision to disband the community, if not exactly inevitable, was certainly the easiest way of dealing with the situation. What is difficult to condone is the way in which the matter was handled.

Fifty years after these events it seems to me that Brother Joseph was comparatively little to blame. His manic temperament seems to have made him at times the victim of a mild paranoia; his conviction that he was now no longer able to continue as the superior at Mount Olivet Monastery was sincere; and it is unlikely that he could have survived as a religious under another superior.

But when he told the Bishop of Southwark in a letter of 8 October 1936 that the other Brothers were 'not sufficiently responsible to carry on with a Superior who would have no knowledge of the work with the boys', I think he did them an injustice. Brother Anthony and Brother Anselm were, in my own judgement, responsible men, who would have worked well under any new superior. Whether Brother Anthony would himself have made a good successor to Brother Joseph is perhaps more *discutable*; perhaps it would have been unfair to have burdened him with so great a responsibility.

At first there was some doubt as to who exactly had the authority to close the monastery and suppress the community. The matter was looked into by two Ramsgate monks who were experts in canon law, and they concluded that this authority rested with the Bishop of Southwark; there was no need of recourse to the Holy See.

The two canonists prepared a lengthy Report, written in Latin, for the guidance of the Bishop. In the Report its authors make some unfavourable comments on the two professed Brothers, but to some extent they safeguard themselves by stating clearly that what they say is based on what the Abbot has told them: '. . . secundum Reverendissimum Patrem Abbatem'.

They record also that the Abbot has told them that in his opinion the Brother Superior is lacking in the spirit of religion: 'quem ceteroquin spiritu religionis plane destitutum putat'. This seems to me a very surprising judgement considering the total support that the Abbot had given to Brother Joseph, and the hard line that he had taken with the other two.

In fact, it looks to me today as if Abbot Taylor was totally at sea about the whole business, and had opted for the easiest way out. Perhaps one can hardly blame him; but it is to be regretted that he handled the affair so clumsily.

After the suppression Brother Anthony was sent to stay for a while at Prinknash Abbey, until the dispensations from vows arrived, Brother Anselm to Farnborough Abbey. At both these religious houses they were kindly received. The Abbot of Prinknash, Dom Wilfrid Upson, knew the realities of the situation; he had visited Mount Olivet; and after Dom Bede Winslow had left, three Prinknash monks were successive chaplains at Frensham. One of these, Dom Benedict Steuart, says in a letter to Brother Anthony (Mr Joseph Bullen) written on 22 July 1941: 'After I left Frensham I heard from Br. Joseph from time to time, but he has not written now for a good time & I have no wish to open correspondence with him again, tho' I would answer if he wrote, of course. The whole business was very sad & I have always regretted that what seemed to me when I first went there such an ideal little community should have been so ruthlessly brought to an end.'

The rescripts cancelling the two professed Brothers' vows were never signed by them. They explained why in a letter to the Archbishop-Bishop of Southwark—Dr Amigo had been created an archbishop *ad personam* by Pius XII—dated 2 March 1939.

> ...We should like to add a word in explanation. Our signatures have not been withheld in any spirit of contumacy or disrespect. As we have already explained to Abbot Taylor: it seems to us that the signing of the document would be in the nature of a signing-away of our interests in the former Congregation and an abandoning of our claim to a financial settlement. We have always accepted the decrees in principle and have intended to sign it [*sic*] as soon as the community's affairs were financially adjusted. The delay is not of our seeking.
>
> We wish also to point out to your Grace the fact that our own view of the state of affairs which led to the dissolution of the Frensham community has never been put before you: because, when one of us last autumn asked Brother Joseph to request Abbot Taylor to make a canonical visitation to inquire into our difficulties, this request was not granted. The Abbot came in order to enforce a decision already made.

The two Brothers had each made a substantial gift of money to the community after taking their vows as Anglicans. Whether they had a strict right in Roman canon law to reimbursement is perhaps doubtful; but that in natural justice, and in charity, they had a clear moral right is certain. This the Archbishop seems to have recognized in principle, and he directed the diocesan financial secretary to look into the matter. But the Mount Olivet finances were in as much confusion as ever. Brother Joseph had managed somehow to clear off debts amounting to £1,500, and was apparently unable to do anything further. The Brothers' claim was never resolved.

After the disbanding of the SCK Joe Bullen (Brother Anthony) worked for a number of years at the Warneford mental hospital in Oxford, where he was much loved and very highly esteemed. In fact, there was much grief at the Warneford when he left, to

71

take up a domestic post at Pusey House. Eventually he returned to his home at Woodbridge, so as to be with his ageing mother. This act of filial devotion, together with the East Anglian climate, seems to have told on him, and after a period of increasing weakness he died on 26 April 1964, at the age of 57. His body rested throughout the night of April 28-29 in the charming little Catholic church of the Holy Family and St Michael the Archangel at Kesgrave, Suffolk. His Requiem Mass was celebrated there at 11.30 a.m. on Wednesday April 29th, the Mass being served by Mr Donald Halliday (formerly Brother Edmund, SCK). The interment followed in the Catholic section of the Woodbridge cemetery.

John Fuller (Brother Anselm) rejoined his father in the family business in Dover. He married happily, and died in the 1970s, leaving one son.

After the break-up of the community at Mount Olivet the Institution for mentally defective boys did not long continue. It seems to have been closed towards the end of 1939.

Once rid of the encumbrance of this community, Brother Joseph soon recovered from his depression. But before the Institution was closed the Circus went on to achieve greater triumphs than ever. During 1939 it attracted enthusiastic audiences in Haslemere, Guildford, Bognor Regis, Winchester, Hayling Island, Ealing, and a number of other places. At Haslemere the Big Top was blown down in a gale, sustaining damage that cost £300 to repair. In the course of the year the Circus was seen by some 15,000 people. With the outbreak of war in September a number of other performances had to be cancelled, and the Circus brought home.

The ever-resourceful Reg Gardner—strictly speaking Brother Joseph had now been reduced to the secular state, though outwardly he gave no sign of this—had quite recovered his old energy, and quickly reopened Mount Olivet as the Thomas More School for Backward Boys. The inmates of the new school were normal boys in all respects except for their inability to pass examinations. There are always plenty of such boys around, and plenty of parents willing handsomely to renumerate anyone who will take them in hand. At this difficult time of transition Brother Joseph was fortunate in being able to recruit to his new staff Mr James Bowery, who came to Frensham from Besford Court. Earlier, he had paid a number of visits to Frensham, and so had seen the excellent conditions under which the work of the Institution was carried on, and the good relations between the staff and boys.

To get the new Thomas More School started it was essential to secure the patronage and support of Archbishop Amigo. Once again Brother Joseph presented himself, by appointment, at Pugin's episcopal palace in St George's Road, SE1. This time he was accompanied by Mr Bowery. For the ex-Brother Superior this interview was crucial. His whole future was at stake. Never lacking in boldness, he was now seeking nothing less than episcopal approval of the new school, and permission for himself to continue to wear the religious habit and style himself 'Brother Joseph'. Also, he was fairly certainly hoping —it was a rather faint hope, one would have thought—that just possibly the Archbishop-Bishop might be willing in some way to help in the solving of the financial problems left by the extinct SCK.

Especially important to him was the matter of permission to appear before the public as a recognized ecclesiastical person. The possibility of his having to appear in the streets of Farnham in lay attire hardly bore thinking about, so great would have been the loss of prestige; and so predictable the reactions of his creditors in the town.

But all went well, and in all respects. The only outward change that followed in Brother Joseph's life-style was that he replaced his grey monastic habit with a black one, made by a tailor in Farnham, as being more in keeping with his status as a Benedictine secular oblate.

One who did not approve of this sartorial restyling was Father Robo, who from this time on never acknowledged Brother Joseph's implied claim to be a religious. In which, of course, strictly speaking, Father Robo was right. But, firm traditionalist as he was, it was not likely that the Reverend Etienne Robo would ever appreciate so original a spiritual *entrepreneur* as Brother Joseph Gard'ner.

The Thomas More School prospered; after the war the Circus was revived, with the boys of the school as the performers, achieving new successes. On 25 July 1947 the following paragraph appeared in the *Farnham Herald*.

Visitors to the Circus

On Tuesday, a convoy of 16 coaches was seen to be passing
through Farnham en route for the Frensham Circus. 600
children from South London spent an exciting day at a special
performance. The scene was repeated on Wednesday, when
four coachloads from different parts arrived at Frensham, and
the Big Top was again filled with more than 600 enthusiastic
circus fans. Many of our local schools, clubs and camps have
arranged visits to the circus this year and an exceptionally fine
programme has been widely appreciated.

A fortnight later Brother Joseph was dead. He died on 8 August
1947, at the age of 39, after quite a short illness; but his health had
been troubling him for some time. The Requiem Mass, celebrated
by Dom Bede Winslow, took place in the chapel of the Thomas
More School— the former Mount Olivet Monastery chapel—and
the burial was in the Roman Catholic portion of the Farnham
public cemetery.

What, I ask myself, do I think of Brother Joseph Gard'ner fifty
years on from the time when I knew him? I knew him at a time
of crisis in his life, when he was under a good deal more strain
than I then realized. As a novice in his community I knew nothing
of the severe financial problems that were besetting him; nor had
I any real idea of the pressures, both internal and external, that
he was under. It is an old and sound monastic principle—though
it seems to be widely disregarded today—that novices should
know nothing of 'the secrets of the convent' (the word convent
here meaning community). But I did know that Brother Anthony
and Brother Anselm were much distressed by Brother Joseph's
seemingly disproportionate involvement with the Circus, to the
detriment of his responsibilities as superior; and I knew that they
were still further worried by his plans for taking the Circus on tour.

The dénouement that overtook the community was sudden and
unexpected. At the time, forgetting the dominical injunction 'Judge
not', I judged Brother Joseph very severely, with all the ununder-
standing of relative youth. Today it would still be wrong to judge;

it is better to try to seek understanding. It seems to me now that Abbot Taylor and Dr Amigo were in their different ways remiss in not seeking to investigate what was really behind the unhappiness in Mount Olivet Monastery; perhaps a convert community of only four men meant little to either of them, and was viewed as expendable once it had run into trouble. Each will have acted for the best, as he saw things; they were scarcely men of insight.

When I first went to Mount Olivet, in 1937, Dom Bede Winslow was still in residence as chaplain. He was an excellent community man, and contributed much to the basically happy, harmonious atmosphere then prevailing. But already the Circus was the uppermost thing in Brother Joseph's mind, and this was beginning to make life difficult for the Brothers. On the whole, though, things seemed to be running smoothly enough. For myself, I found Brother Joseph kind and considerate; he took care to see that I had work that I would find congenial; in fact, I was virtually the editor of the last two numbers of *Christus Rex*.

Certainly Brother Joseph was temperamental; he was easily irritated, and the boys went in some awe of his rages. Generally speaking, however, he was good company; he was an entertaining and amusing conversationalist, and a splendid *raconteur*, with a rich store of anecdote. His wit, it must be admitted, was inclined to be barbed, often at the expense of Anglican clergymen and bishops he had known. He was an excellent mimic. Our evening community recreations, taken over cups of tea at a long refectory-style table in the library, could be very enjoyable. It would not be quite correct to say that Brother Joseph dominated these informal proceedings, but he was certainly their life and soul. I do not remember him ever breaking into song, but he had a good collection of records of different kinds of music, both sacred and profane, and these he used to play to us on the large radio-gramophone that stood in the library. One record that he particularly enjoyed, and we enjoyed it too, was of that classic folk-song 'Turmut-hoeing', with its rousing chorus:

For the fly, the fly, the fly be on the turmut;
And it's all my eye for we to try to keep fly off the turmut.

Another favourite record of his was of a popular song of the day, 'Old Potato Jones', of which I can remember only the refrain:

Old Potato Jones—
He's a sterling son of the sea,
The finest skipper you ever did see:
Old Potato Jones (etc., etc.).

'Potato' Jones was a mariner who achieved a temporary fame in the 1930s by his gun-running exploits during the Spanish civil war.

Joseph Gard'ner's attempt to found a religious community was a gallant effort. How he got the idea remains unknown; but he must have been sincere; otherwise he would never have put up with the hardships and mortifications that he encountered at Staithes and Pershore. This was all the more to his credit because of his very poor health. But the religious life was something to which he was not really suited, and for which he had never been trained in any normal way. Essentially he was by temperament an actor, showman, and impresario; these elements in his character he was never able to subdue. He had a great way with boys, and his institution for mental defectives was a distinct success, culminating as it did in the foundation of the Frensham Circus. But over the Circus he drove himself too hard; under the strain some kind of psycho-physical breakdown was inevitable.

His enduring achievement and lasting monument is the More House School, as it is now called. One of its specific functions is still to educate those boys at Secondary Level whose attainments fall short of their potential. In the school Brother Joseph's memory is held in high regard, as the Founder: and rightly so.

Dom Simon Bowery, Father Charles Borelli (of the well known Farnham family of that name), and others who knew him well, have only happy memories of him. As a writer in *The Southwark Record* put it some years after his death: 'Brother Joseph's genius lay more in his youth work and in running a "one man show" than in presiding over a Catholic community under a Rule.' In many ways he was ahead of his time. He started life with few advantages and a number of handicaps. Perhaps his fault was that he was in too much of a hurry, and tried to do too much. He was a man who played many parts, some more successfully than others. No one who knew him could ever forget him.

APPENDIX I

Members of the Congregation of Servants of Christ the King

Founder, Superior and Novice Master: The Reverend Brother
Joseph (Reginald) Gard'ner

Brother Francis (Joseph) Wilson. At Staithes, Pershore, and Frensham. Later married.

Brother Ignatius of the Passion. Possibly at Staithes; Pershore and Frensham. Dismissed by the Superior.

Brother Bernard Plant. At Pershore. Left after the move to Frensham. Went to Australia; later in Anglican orders.

Brother Dominic Williamson. At Pershore. Left from Frensham to become Roman Catholic. Spent the rest of his life as a laybrother at St Augustine's Abbey, Ramsgate (OSB).

Brother Benedict Hinton (†1988). Left from Frensham, and thereafter worked for the London publishers and booksellers, Messrs Burns Oates.

Brother Anthony (Joseph Reginald) Bullen. Dispensed from vows after the dissolution of the community in 1938.

Brother Anselm (Godfrey John) Fuller. Ditto. Subsequently married.

Brother Edmund (Donald) Halliday. Novice at <u>Mount Olivet</u>. Left in 1938. Merchant Navy service during the war. Subsequently a conventual oblate at Belmont Abbey (OSB), Hereford, until retirement through ill health.

Brother Louis Lailavoix. Novice at Mount Olivet, 1937-38. Of French nationality. Called up for the French Army, 1939. Later discharged from the Army through ill health. Attempted during the war, with the encouragement of a friendly priest, to found a Franciscan third order brotherhood in a bombed house in Canning Town, E. London.

Brother Aelred (Michael) Sewell. Novice, 1937-38. Dismissed at dissolution of the community. Entered the Carmelite Order, 1952, after previous studies with the Canons Regular of the Lateran. Ordained priest, 1954.

Brother Martin (Wilfrid Hall). At Pershore and Frensham. *Familiaris*. Secretary and chauffeur to Brother Joseph. Left, in the 1930s. Now (1986) Overseer at Trinity Hospital, Retford, Notts.

Chaplains at Mount Olivet Monastery

The Reverend William Francis Wyber (Anglican)
Dom Bede Winslow, OSB (St Augustine's Abbey, Ramsgate)
Dom Ambrose Holly, OSB (Prinknash Abbey, Gloucester)
Dom Benedict Steuart, OSB (Prinknash Abbey)
Dom Brendan McHugh, OSB (Prinknash Abbey)
Dom Urban Rouvière, OSB (St Augustine's Abbey, Ramsgate)

APPENDIX II

THE REVEREND W.F. WYBER

I knew Father Wyber during the time he was chaplain to the Sisters of St John the Evangelist at Sandymount, Dublin, and after he left until his death in England.

Before coming to Ireland he was chaplain to the Servants of Christ the King in Surrey until they went over to Rome. He remained with them until they got a new chaplain. Up till then he continued to say Mass on weekdays in the chapel of Mount Olivet Monastery, and a visiting Roman priest officiated on Sundays! He always spoke of the Brothers and the boys they looked after with affection.

Father Wyber was not an easy person to get to know as he was rather remote, shy, and humble, with a wry sense of humour and a friendly smile. He had the same silent laugh as Archbishop John Charles (Dr McQuaid) of Dublin; indeed in many ways he reminded me of him. He also had the same unbending attitude concerning the teachings of Holy Church.

He seemed to spend much of the day in prayer; when he went into the city he always visited St Teresa's, Clarendon Street, the church of the Discalced Carmelite Fathers. He seemed to prefer Latin to English in church services. He always read his Office in Latin, and he used Latin for the priest's prayers of preparation for Mass. He never spoke before he had finished his thanksgiving after Mass each morning; but after I had left for Trinity College, Dublin, it was only in the evening that I got a chance to chat to him.

On Sundays he spent the time between the early Low Mass and the later Sung Mass kneeling in silent prayer on the sacristy floor. He was a very holy man indeed, a saint with a great affection for St Francis, and indeed all the saints; but he had a special devotion to a rather obscure, to me at any rate, Polish saint, Stanislaus Kostka. He was the sort of person you would want to have beside you when you were about to die, because he seemed to walk close to God. Perhaps he should have been a Carthusian or Cistercian.

Apart from an annual journey to Chester, to go into retreat, he remained here in Dublin until his final departure in 1940. His last Mass in Ireland was celebrated in Latin at the Lady altar in St John's Convent. When I brought him to the mail boat I asked him for a photograph of himself; but he remarked, with his wry smile, that photographs were not necessary to remember one's friends by.

The only way I can describe what he seemed to feel when he left Ireland is to use the Portuguese word *saudades*. He went as chaplain to a small community in Essex, and when he died the Matron sent me some of his few worldly possessions.

In 1939 my sister was operated on for a sarcoma. After the operation her temperature began to rise; they were unable to bring it down, and said that there was nothing more they could do. It was, they said, only a question of time.

I asked Father Wyber to offer the Mass for the Dying, but instead he celebrated the Mass of the Holy Guardian Angels. During the Mass the blood-clot which had been causing the rise in temperature dispersed. My sister is now a happily married, energetic woman of sixty.

Other facets of Father Wyber's character were charity and compassion.

Let it be said of him: *Tu es sacerdos in aeternum secundum ordinem Melchisedech.*

Ronald Anderson

APPENDIX III

In the last three months of 1930 Brother Joseph preached on behalf of his fraternity at the following churches: St Bartholomew's, St Luke's, St Mary's, and Holy Trinity, Reading; St Margaret's, and St Stephen's, Liverpool; St Alban's, and St. Benedict's, Manchester; St Mary Magdalene's, and St Columba's, Sunderland; All Saints, Evesham; St Martin's, Worcester; Loftus Parish Church; Saltburn Parish Church; St Sampson's, and All Saints, York; St Thomas's, New Marske; St Mary's, Thorpe; St Mary's, Ilford; St Peter's, Clapham; St Magnus the Martyr, St Andrew-by-the-Wardrobe, and St Martin's, Ludgate (all in the City of London).

In the same three months he addressed meetings in Loftus, York, Reading, and London, and spoke at the annual general meeting of the Guild of Servants of the Sanctuary, at Church House, Westminster, and at the annual festival of the Guild's Sunderland Chapter, at St Columba's, Sunderland.

Christus Rex for January 1931—the magazine's first number—adds that 'He now hopes for a little rest and retirement.'

The writer of this report—probably Brother Joseph himself—adds that: 'Everywhere, people showed great interest and kindness, and we are grateful to all concerned—more especially to the clergy who have opened their pulpits to us. This sort of preaching seems to be necessary in view of the widespread ignorance concerning the Religious Life of the English Church; but while we thus speak of the external part of the Religious State, the Life itself must be kept hidden, and we hope it will be made possible for us to live the Life and concentrate on our novitiate without constant public appeals.'

THIS BOOK
IS PUBLISHED BY
THE AYLESFORD PRESS
158 MORETON ROAD, UPTON, WIRRAL, CHESHIRE

IT IS SET IN 12-POINT LINOTYPE GRANJON
PRINTED BY
BLOOMFIELD AND SON, GROVE ROAD, STRATFORD-UPON-AVON
ON ANTIQUE LAID PAPER,
AND BOUND BY
THOMAS LOUGHLIN, CANNING PLACE, LIVERPOOL.

THE ORDINARY EDITION
IS BOUND INTO PAPER COVERS.
THE DE LUXE EDITION
OF 33 COPIES, OF WHICH 25 ARE FOR SALE,
IS BOUND IN QUARTER LINSON
WITH DECORATIVE PAPER SIDES.
THEY ARE NUMBERED
AND SIGNED BY THE AUTHOR.